PLAS

PITT
LATIN
AMERICAN
SERIES

Discreet Partners

DISCREET PARTNERS

Argentina and the USSR since 1917

Aldo César Vacs

Translated by Michael Joyce

UNIVERSITY OF PITTSBURGH PRESS

Published by the University of Pittsburgh Press, Pittsburgh, Pa. 15260
Copyright © 1984, University of Pittsburgh Press
All rights reserved
Feffer and Simons, Inc., London
Manufactured in the United States of America

Library of Congress Cataloging in Publication Data

Vacs, Aldo César.
  Discreet partners.

  (Pitt Latin American series)
  Translation of: Los socios discretos.
  Bibliography: p. 143.
  Includes index.
  1. Argentina—Relations—Soviet Union. 2. Soviet Union—
Relations—Argentina. I. Title. II. Series.
F2833.5.S65V3213 1984   327.82047   84-3496
ISBN 0-8229-1143-4

*The translation of this book was made possible
by the generous support of the Latin American Studies Program
of the University of Pittsburgh's Center for International Studies.*

For my parents and Trudi

Contents

Tables

Acknowledgments

• This book is a slightly modified version of a study conducted during 1981 and 1982 under the auspices of the Tinker Foundation and the Latin American Studies Program of the University of Pittsburgh's Center for International Studies. Various persons and institutions offered me the support necessary to undertake the project and finish it in good time.

The generous financial assistance of the Tinker Foundation gave me both the time and the material means to devote full effort to the writing of this book. I am all the more indebted because the Tinker Fellowship program is one of the few that permits Latin American scholars to study and conduct research in the United States while they are still in training.

The University of Pittsburgh's Latin American Studies Program was extremely generous in its assistance. Its director, Carmelo Mesa-Lago, its assistant director, Alan Adelman, and its staff, June Belkin, José Cisneros, Linda Gaskill, Shirley Kregar, Marci Valle, and Kay Wilson, offered me not only the use of the center's facilities but also unflagging friendship, cordiality, and understanding.

Even before my arrival in Pittsburgh, Professor Cole Blasier was strongly supportive of this project. A tireless adviser and a man of great dedication and courtesy, he shared with me his wide knowledge; this book has benefited immeasurably from his astute comments, suggestions, and critical observations. To him goes much of the credit for whatever merits it might display.

I owe a similar debt of gratitude to Professor Reid Andrews. Our discussions over the past two years have provided fresh insights on the topic, and his comments led to many improvements in the manuscript.

Eduardo Lozano, Latin American bibliographer of the Hillman Library, University of Pittsburgh, greatly eased my labors in gathering materials and data, and his friendship made this period one of the most fruitful in my life.

Michael Joyce's enthusiastic contribution far exceeded a mere translation of the manuscript. I am deeply grateful for his efforts to make it more succinct and readable, and for providing excellent advice in order to improve substantial aspects of it.

As editor Jane Flanders offered many acute and precise observations that helped to improve greatly the quality of the final version, both in style and content.

Many friends in Latin America and the United States, through their interest and encouragement, cemented my commitment to this project; I thank them for their many kindnesses over the years.

My parents and Trudi were always close to me with their affection and understanding, and their steady support made this undertaking far easier than it otherwise would have been. This book is dedicated to them for having encouraged me to pursue a career in the social sciences and, above all, for having been pillars of support whenever difficulties presented themselves.

Obviously, none of the institutions and persons mentioned is responsible for the opinions offered in this book or for any errors it might contain, but I hope the final product presented here fulfills—at least in part—the expectations of all those who assisted in its completion.

Introduction

• Since the early 1970s, the character of Argentine-Soviet relations has undergone fundamental change as bilateral ties have increased and deepened. Analysts in academia, government, and international organizations have only recently begun to assess the possible consequences of this new phenomenon.

Argentine-Soviet rapprochement is of particular interest because, for most of the twentieth century, Argentina's ruling groups have been openly hostile to the Soviet Union and communism, on both the domestic and international level. Argentine governments, especially military governments, continue to regard the Marxist-Leninist ideology espoused by the Soviet leadership as a powerful enemy that must be resisted, both ideologically and militarily.

On the domestic level, Argentine governments have attacked, more or less violently, groups adopting a communist and/or pro-Soviet stance. In the international arena, most governments have proclaimed Argentina's membership in a "Western and Christian world" that must be defended—at least rhetorically—against "communists and atheists."

Relations between Argentina and the USSR could thus be expected to be very cold or very tense, if they existed at all. By all rights, Argentina should regard the Soviet Union as a dangerous enemy, while the Soviets should characterize Argentina as fascist or semifascist. But, however true this was in the past, the present reality is quite different.

Both countries are currently major trading partners. The majority of Argentina's meat and grain exports are now destined for the Soviet market, and medium-term agreements on continued supply have been negotiated. The Soviets, for their part, have established a foothold in the Argentine market through sales of equipment and machinery, especially electricity-generating equipment, and both parties expect trade to expand and diversify. Agreements on economic and scientific-technical cooperation have further cemented bilateral ties.

In the diplomatic sphere, both countries have virtually ceased their verbal attacks on each other and appear to be moving toward a tacit alliance in international forums. This new cordiality originated in the Soviets' defense of Argentina's human rights record and Argentina's refusal to join the 1980 grain embargo, and was consolidated during the 1982 Malvinas crisis.

Although military contacts have remained extremely discreet, military delegations have exchanged visits, and military attachés have been posted in Moscow and Buenos Aires. The USSR has also begun to supply Argentina with nuclear material for the latter's nuclear development program. Although no arms sales have been made, the weapons shortage created by the Malvinas crisis might change the situation; in any case, training and technical assistance are likely to increase.

Expanded relations have affected Argentine society and politics, favoring the emergence and consolidation of sectors that benefit from ties with the USSR and promote their continuation and growth.

This situation, in which the forging of ever closer ties seems to contradict the ideology and ultimate objectives that both countries claim to uphold, has given rise to diverse reactions and interpretations. At the extremes, some observers regard relations as limited purely to the economic plane, while others see the formation of an Argentine-Soviet alliance.

But neither of these two positions, nor any variations in between, has been argued with sufficient clarity or rests on an adequate empirical foundation. It was for this reason this book was written, to explore the characteristics of the Argentine-Soviet relationship and to assess, to the greatest extent possible, its causes and probable future developments.

The primary objective of this book is to provide an adequate empirical foundation on which to base interpretations of Argentine-Soviet relations. Up to now, no study of these relations in their totality has been undertaken, although partial studies, especially of economic matters, do exist. At least two factors have contributed to the absence of empirically based research on the topic: its relative novelty and the persistent tendency of some analysts to study the Argentine-Soviet relationship from a "geopolitical" perspective which, in disregarding data, necessarily implies an a priori bias for or against the relationship and thereby prevents an objective understanding of the phenomenon.

This study focuses on the Argentine side of the relationship, and only secondarily on the Soviet, for it has been the changing political, social, and economic circumstances in Argentina that have determined the cycles of rapprochement and rejection between the two countries. The position of the USSR, by contrast, has been almost invariably in favor of rapprochement, and Soviet foreign policy has been less directly affected by changes in the domestic situation.

The main hypothesis of this book is that Argentine-Soviet relations are based on complementary needs in trade and production. Other bilateral ties have been built on this foundation of shared economic interests. However, the economic factor is but one of several in the relationship. Diplomatic and military ties, although developed later than economic ones, are gradually increasing in importance. These new converging interests must be studied by assessing their importance and analyzing their (not always economic) causes, if we are to arrive at a comprehensive picture of the relationship that is both explicative and predictive.

Furthermore, the relationship with the Soviet Union has had a number of important effects on Argentine society. Two of the most significant have been the emergence of powerful socioeconomic groups in favor of maintaining ties with the USSR, and the changed role of the Partido Comunista Argentino, which, in a break with tradition, achieved a modus vivendi with a military government.

The validity of these impressions will be tested throughout this book, which begins with a review of the historical evolution of Argentine-Soviet relations up to 1970. The following chapters describe and analyze the economic, diplomatic, and military aspects of these relations, as well as their social and political impact on Argentina, since the early 1970s. Thus equipped with the proper tools for correctly interpreting the causes and probable effects of bilateral ties, we can attempt to penetrate the reserve demonstrated by both actors in this discreet partnership.

Discreet Partners

1 Intermittent Ties: Argentina and the Soviet Union, 1917–1970

• Difficult Beginnings

When militant Bolsheviks attacked foreign legations in Moscow and Petrograd in June 1918, only two were spared, those of Argentina and Persia, probably out of sympathy with their "semicolonial" status.[1] Despite this seemingly propitious beginning, relations between Argentina and the Soviet Union were soon to become troubled.

Not long afterward, the Argentine legation in Petrograd was seized, and the honorary consul, J. Navellian, was arrested on charges of espionage; subjected to harsh and humiliating treatment, he was not allowed to leave the USSR until 1920.[2] The Argentine government subsequently followed a hard line, not only refusing to recognize the Soviet Union, but also adding insult to injury by continuing to recognize Eugene Stein, an appointee of Kerenski's provisional government, as Russia's official representative until 1928.[3] Soviet protests, such as that of Maxim Litvinov in April 1923 objecting to the activities of "Ambassador Stein" and proposing the establishment of direct relations, were ignored.[4]

The Soviets continued probing for a diplomatic opening throughout the mid-1920s. Chicherin and Litvinov publicly declared interest in friendly relations on a number of occasions, and the Soviet representatives in Germany and Italy tried to initiate talks with their Argentine counterparts in 1925.[5] The Argentine government firmly rejected all Soviet attempts at rapprochement, however, stating simply that it had no interest in establishing relations with the regime it held responsible for the attack on the legation.

• The Initiation of Trade

Argentina's repeated refusal to discuss the opening of diplomatic relations did not prevent commercial ties from developing by the mid-1920s. In November 1925 Boris Kraevsky, a representative of the Soviet trade office for North America, Amtorg, was sent to Buenos Aires to purchase hides and explore possibilities in the Argentine market. Granted a fairly free rein by the Soviet government, Kraevsky obtained a trading license from the Argentine government and soon expanded his field of operations to include the entire River Plate region and Chile.[6]

Under Kraevsky's dynamic management, the Buenos Aires office was successful in dramatically increasing the volume of trade between the two countries, although Argentine exports to the USSR always far exceeded Soviet sales to Argentina (see table 1). At the same time, Kraevsky opened some political doors by hiring Dr. Mario Guido, a Radical politician and president of the Chamber of Deputies, as attorney for the commercial office.[7]

The rapid growth of the Buenos Aires office led to its separation from Amtorg and its reorganization as a separate Soviet trade office for South America—Yuzhamtorg—in November 1927.[8] The closing of the Soviet trade office in London, Arcos, in May 1927 was probably an additional factor in the decision to detach Soviet commercial activities in South America from Amtorg's North American operations. Yuzhamtorg was legally recognized by the Argentine government in December 1927, and the volume of trade rose meteorically—including the level of

Table 1
Soviet Trade with Argentina 1923–1930
(in thousands of rubles)

	Exports	Imports
1923–24	—	4,674
1924–25	—	37,099
1925–26	3	36,304
1927	1,157	89,672
1928	2,737	29,836
1929	12,947	98,928
1930	12,864	60,522

Sources: Latinskaya Amerika, p. 83, Clissold, *Soviet Relations*, p. 9.

Soviet exports to Argentina (see figures for 1929 in table 1). This increase was probably related to a commercial exposition of Soviet products held in Buenos Aires in September and October 1928. Organized by Yuzhamtorg, the exposition featured petroleum products, chemical salts, coal, films, wood, and handicrafts. It attracted, Kraevsky estimated, more than a hundred thousand visitors.[9]

The most important aspect of the expansion of Soviet exports was a plan, never fully implemented, to sell petroleum products and gasoline at prices below those of the international market dominated by English and American companies. Western suppliers reacted violently, accusing the Soviets of dumping. Some observers claim this trade deal was one of the reasons for the military coup of 1930.[10] According to Soviet sources, during this period the major Argentine exports were hides, wool, tannin, and livestock, while Soviet exports consisted largely of petroleum, coal, cement, and chemical and manufactured products in limited quantities.[11]

The diplomatic situation was far less favorable to the USSR. Although the president of Argentina from 1922 to 1928, Marcelo T. de Alvear, was a member of the Unión Cívica Radical (UCR), a nationalist party based in the middle and lower classes, he was more moderate and less inclined to innovation in foreign relations than his predecessor, Hipólito Yrigoyen. In 1928, however, the Alvear era ended with Yrigoyen's reelection, raising Soviet hopes that the old caudillo, who had displayed an anticolonialist and anti-imperialist spirit during his first presidency, would be inclined to recognize the Soviet Union.[12]

These expectations came to naught when Yrigoyen refused to grant diplomatic recognition to the USSR. This refusal was probably the result of an unfavorable report issued shortly before Yrigoyen's inauguration by Alvear's foreign minister, Angel Gallardo; the report referred to the 1918 attack on the Argentine legation in Petrograd and the subsequent arrest of the consul as an affront to "the dignity of the republic," and warned of the dangers of the expansion of communism.[13] But commercial relations between the two countries continued to develop satisfactorily. The only important changes were Kraevsky's replacement by Alexander Minkin as head of the Soviet delegation and the hiring of another influential Radical, Honorio Pueyrredón, to replace Guido as attorney for Yuzhamtorg.[14]

• The Closing of Yuzhamtorg and the Rupture of Relations

In September 1930 the Yrigoyen government was overthrown by a military coup under the command of General José Félix Uriburu, whose two-year regime displayed marked anticommunist and profascist tendencies.[15] Yuzhamtorg at first attempted to ignore the political implications of the coup and, in a display of pragmatism, sought to expand its operations by offering the government an advantageous trade deal for the importation of Soviet petroleum at prices below those of the international market. This proposal in effect amounted to a return to the barter system. The Soviets offered to purchase Argentine hides, cotton, tannin, and above all livestock (to compensate for herds destroyed by the kulaks in resistance to collectivization) in amounts exactly equal to the worth of the petroleum imported.[16] After some hesitation, however, the Argentine government rejected the proposal, a decision that has been subject to differing interpretations. One school of thought credits the Uriburu regime with acting in the national interest to prevent bankruptcies and unemployment in the Argentine oil industry,[17] while another attributes the rejection to the pressure of British and North American interests closely associated with the government.[18]

A few months after this rebuff, on 31 July 1931, Argentine police raided the Yuzhamtorg office in Buenos Aires, arrested its entire staff (with the exception of Minkin, who was in Montevideo), and proceeded to close its other Argentine field offices. The Soviet firm was accused of conducting "economic warfare against Argentine importers by means of widespread dumping of non-Russian goods," "working to the detriment of Argentine industry," and "promoting communism."[19] The first two accusations had little enough basis in fact—or were at least a matter of opinion—but the lattermost charge was entirely groundless. An intensive search of Yuzhamtorg's archives undertaken with the assistance of Russian emigrés resident in Argentina with little sympathy for the Soviet Union merely turned up evidence of the existence of a section of the NKVD (probably to oversee the conduct of functionaries and prevent defections), a number of safe-conduct passes for entering the USSR (necessitated by the absence of a Soviet diplomatic legation in Argentina), some propaganda materials on the first Five Year Plan, and the use of an elaborate code (necessary to preserve commercial secrets). Nevertheless, nothing was found to substantiate any direct connection between Yuzhamtorg and the Comintern or local communists, and no charges of espionage were made.[20] The accusation that Yuzhamtorg was used to finance the activities of other Latin American parties, made, among others, by Richard Krebs (alias Jean Valtin), also turned out to be weak.[21] Argentine police reports indicated that Kraevsky was extremely careful in his contacts, if they existed at all, and that money was transferred from the USSR via Comintern channels and not through Soviet commercial offices.[22]

The Soviet reaction to the closing of Yuzhamtorg was surprisingly mild; it was limited to the publication of an article in *Pravda* attributing the closing to imperialist pressure from Great Britain and the United States and the military government's need to find a "scapegoat" for internal economic problems.[23] Yuzhamtorg's central offices were transferred to Montevideo in short order. In December 1931 an advertisement was published in *La Nación* detailing the economic advantages that relations with the USSR had represented for Argentina and petitioning for the reopening of Yuzhamtorg, a request rejected by the Uriburu government. In October 1932 the Soviets finally abandoned all hope of reestablishing commercial ties and liquidated Yuzhamtorg's operations in Buenos Aires.[24]

This first chapter in Argentine-Soviet relations established a pattern that has remained virtually intact almost up to the present. First, economic relations have always outweighed diplomatic and political considerations. The two countries have continued to trade despite their ideological and political differences, and trading relations have been disrupted only when powerful economic interests considered themselves adversely affected. Second, the balance of trade has almost always been negative for the Soviets (the only exceptions being the years 1955 – 56 and 1958 – 59, when the balance was negative for Argentina). The habitual Soviet deficit is the result of a nonreciprocal trading pattern in which the Soviet Union imports large quantities of Argentine primary products to compensate for deficiencies in its own agricultural sector, while Argentina traditionally relies on Western markets for its imported goods.

Also important is the pragmatism demonstrated by the Soviet Union and the care it has taken to prevent political and ideological differences from disrupting normal trading relations. The USSR established its commercial offices in Buenos Aires despite the Argentine government's continued recognition of the "tsarist" representative; waited patiently in the hope that Yrigoyen's return to the presidency would lead to the establishment of diplomatic relations and ignored the rebuff when no rapprochement occurred; refrained from directly financing Argentine communists and organizations allied with them; limited its propaganda efforts to promoting increased trade rather than improving the image of the USSR or spreading communism; and, finally, continued making conciliatory gestures even after the installation of Uriburu's right-wing military government and the violent closing of Yuzhamtorg's offices in 1932.

Soviet flexibility is grounded on a very concrete need for a reliable supplier of agricultural products, but it also reflects a long-term political calculation. While perhaps not so optimistic as to expect an Argentine alignment with the USSR, the Soviets have always hoped that the tensions arising from Argentina's dependence on Great Britain (and later, the United States) would lead to its withdrawal from the Western sphere of influence. The Soviets are thus always ready to encourage any Argentine moves toward rapprochement.

Argentina, on the other hand, has alternated between rapprochement and rejection of the Soviets, largely due to the different ideologies of various civilian and military governments. This relative lack of interest in relations with the Soviet Union could be explained—at least until 1945—by Argentina's political and economic dependence on Britain and, secondarily, on the United States and the rest of Europe. The majority of Argentine exports were destined for these countries, and relations with Britain were so close that commercial treaties had converted Argentina into the "Sixth Dominion"—as economically dependent on Britain as were Canada or Australia.[25] Conversely, most Argentine imports came from in Western Europe and North America, and Argentine governments saw little need to diversify their purchases abroad. This relatively stable situation did not begin to deteriorate until the economic crisis of the 1930s and proved impossible to maintain after the restructuring of the international economic order after World War II.

For a number of reasons, the Partido Comunista Argentino (PCA) has had virtually no role to play in Argentine-Soviet relations, which have always taken the form of intergovernmental contacts or contacts between Soviet organizations and private Argentine interests — to the exclusion of the PCA and the rest of the Argentine left. Although the PCA was the first communist party in Latin America — it was formed after a split in the Partido Socialista in 1918 and adopted its present name in 1920 — its small membership and recurrent factionalism have rendered it an unimportant factor in Argentine political life.[26] It is likely, however, that PCA propaganda activities have succeeded in marginally improving the Soviet image among centrists and leftists.

• The Freezing of Relations

In 1932 Uriburu was persuaded by his military colleagues to step aside and restore a semblance of constitutional government. For the next eleven years Argentina was ruled by a succession of conservative governments whose hold on power was guaranteed by rigged elections. With the exception of a brief episode in 1934, the presidential administrations of Agustín P. Justo, Roberto M. Ortiz, and Ramón S. Castillo all pursued a policy of confrontation with the USSR.

Faced with the collapse of traditional markets in Europe, in 1934 the Justo administration sought an economic rapprochement with the Soviet Union that might have led to the reopening of Yuzhamtorg in Buenos Aires. But the determined opposition of some groups in Congress killed the proposal, and relations again became overtly hostile.[27]

Another episode in 1934 was more typical of Argentine intransigence: the Argentine delegation to the League of Nations abstained from voting on a resolution admitting the Soviet Union to the organization because of the "impossibility of [Argentina's] acting under conditions of perfect impartiality," a probable reference to the old dispute concerning the attack on the legation in Petrograd.[28] In 1936 the Argentine delegation to the League justified its refusal to recognize the Soviet Union by explicitly mentioning the legation attack.[29]

Argentine hostility seemed to reach a high point in December 1939 when the foreign minister, José María Cantilo, sent a telegram to the secretary-general of the League proposing the expulsion of the Soviet Union because of its attack on Finland and because it promoted the "creation of fronts inside other countries for the purpose of facilitating the spread of communism."[30]

For the first few years of World War II, Argentina and the Soviet Union were content to ignore each other. Deferring to Argentina's role as a supplier of foodstuffs to Great Britain, the USSR abstained from criticizing a government that apparently sympathized with the Axis, a tilt that became even more pronounced when Castillo, an undisguised admirer of Mussolini's Italy, assumed the presidency and pursued a "neutralist" foreign policy.

Soviet reticence ended when the military coup of June 1943 brought to power a group of profascist officers openly sympathetic to the Axis.[31] As it became obvious that an Allied victory was in sight, the United States and the USSR began to exert pressure on Argentina, the United States by attempting to force the government to take an active position against Germany and Japan (by breaking relations and declaring war), the Soviet Union by preventing any U.S. or Latin American agreement that would give Argentina, although a last-minute ally, the same rights as the other victorious countries in the postwar international order.

Soviet strategy consisted of denouncing the profascist character of the Argentine government and openly aiding the opposition activities of the PCA. In August 1944 the Soviet press published an article denouncing the most powerful group within the army (Grupo de Oficiales Unidos, GOU), and specifically the minister of war, Juan D. Perón, as Nazi agents. The article pointed out that "Hitler's plan for the penetration of Latin America is wholly based on the special position of Argentina and on the calculation of exploiting, on the one hand, the absence of close links between her and the United States, and on the other hand, on certain great-power ambitions harboured by Argentina's ruling circles."[32]

Interestingly, this Soviet analysis explicitly noted the weakness of ties between Argentina and the United States, and Argentina's greater dependence on Great Britain and Europe. The Soviet Union was clearly laying the groundwork for its postwar foreign policy toward Argentina, calculated to take advantage of the Axis defeat, Britain's weakness, and the looming rivalry between itself and the United States.

For the time being, however, the Soviets used Argentina's conduct during the war as a bargaining chip in wrenching concessions from their allies. Toward the end of the conflict and after having convinced Argentina to declare war on the Axis (on Japan for having attacked an American nation and on Germany for being allied with an aggressor), the United States continued applying pressure on the military government through the activities of Ambassador Spruille Braden in Buenos Aires.[33] But in the end the United States, responding to pressure from the other Latin American countries and concerned with establishing a solid hemispheric bloc in preparation for an eventual conflict with the Soviets, decided not to oppose Argentina's admission as a founding member of the United Nations. The United States was supported in this decision by Great Britain, which had accumulated a large debt to Argentina in the course of the war and continued to rely on its agricultural exports. The USSR took advantage of this situation, and having succeeded in gaining the admission of Bielorussia and the Ukraine as full members of the organization, also attempted to gain the admission of the pro-Soviet Polish government installed in Lublin.

Although the Western Allies did not concede this last Soviet demand, the weakness of the Western position with regard to Argentina's behavior during the war not only made it easy for the USSR to gain support for the admission of the two Soviet republics, but also provided an effective propaganda weapon against the other powers at the United Nations.[34] In a speech at the inaugural conference in San Francisco, Molotov stressed that he considered it an injustice to "forget the sins of Argentina" during the war while at the same time "forget[ting] Polish services" to the Allied cause. He obviously neglected to mention that the Western Allies were not blocking Poland's membership per se, but were engaged in a dispute with the Soviet Union over whether to admit the Lublin government or the government-in-exile in London.[35]

A short time later, in June 1945, the Soviet press used the situation in San Francisco to criticize the United States, Great Britain, and other Allied countries for having aided Argentina even though, according to the Soviets, "Argentina's declaration of war on Germany was nothing but a tactical manoeuvre made in agreement with the Hitlerites." In the Soviet view, the Western countries were following a policy of "appeasement" of fascism reminiscent of the prewar era.[36]

• Diplomatic and Economic Openings During the Peronist Era

The immediate postwar era witnessed profound changes in Argentine politics, society, and economics. Pressures exerted by civil society forced the military government to announce that it would relinquish power and convene general elections, and the Peronist movement, whose wide base of popular support had been revealed in a mass demonstration on 17 October 1945, emerged as a serious challenge to the military dictatorship via the ballot box. The elections, which were held in February 1946, were essentially a contest between the Unión Democrática (a united front of the Unión Cívica Radical, the Partido Socialista, the Partido Demócrata Progresista, the PCA, and other minor groups) and the Peronist coalition (consisting principally of the Partido Laborista and the Unión Cívica Radical–Junta Renovadora). The Peronist margin of victory was not very wide, but due to the idiosyncracies of the Argentine electoral system Peronists won the presidency, elected majorities in both houses of Congress, and gained control of the provincial governments.

Up to this point the USSR had been openly hostile to Perón and hopeful that the Unión Democrática, whose members included the recently legalized PCA, would emerge victorious. It now began to reevaluate its position. Recognizing the solid social bases of the Peronist phenomenon and anticipating the Peronists' long hold on power, the Soviets began to alter their strategy, opening the possibility of a rapprochement that would erase previous sources of friction. Perón, recognizing that the USSR was now a major power, had promised to grant it diplomatic recognition during his election campaign. It thus came as no surprise when a joint communique of 6 June 1946—two

days after Perón had assumed the presidency—announced the establishment of diplomatic relations.[37]

The USSR presented this about-face in its position as a demonstration
of the Soviets' desire to contribute to world peace by maintaining
friendly relations with all countries; they suggested that the Argentine
proposal to open relations had resulted from pressures exerted on the
Peronist government by the population,[38] even though there was no
concrete evidence of popular pressure except for the declarations of the
PCA. The Argentine foreign minister, Juan Atilio Bramuglia, told Congress in September 1946 that the opening of relations was a "legal
obligation" that reflected "the desires of the popular masses and the
aspirations of all Argentines, which is to live in peace and friendship
with all nations of the world" and to avoid the international isolation of
Argentina.[39] The new Argentine ambassador to Moscow, Federico
Cantoni, a politician from San Juan Province and a member of the
Peronist front, was more explicitly enthusiastic. He declared before his
departure that he was traveling "to that gigantic laboratory, the Soviet
Union, to observe its development and progress"; and, he continued,
"To make sure that observation is complete and successful, I will be
accompanied by a large group of technicians from different fields,"
adding that "this will lead to the strengthening of economic, scientific,
and political ties with the Soviet Union, [because] under no circumstances ought we to view the Soviet Union as a menace."[40]

Nevertheless, throughout Perón's first term of office (1946–52),
relations with the USSR were not particularly cordial. Argentina's
response to the cold war was not to break off relations, as did Chile and
Brazil, but to engage in occasional rhetorical attacks as proof of its anti-
Sovietism. Two different motives lay behind the ambivalent attitude of
the Peronist government. First, the nationalist-populist character of
Peronism was expressed in foreign policy by the doctrine of the "Third
Position," a kind of avant-garde Third-Worldism which held that Argentina should stand apart from superpower conflicts, avoid integration
in either of the blocs then emerging, and exploit East-West rivalry to
gain political and economic advantages that would permit it to pursue its
aspirations toward leadership of Latin America.[41] Second, whatever
Argentina's intentions, and however eager the Soviet Union may have

been to assist in fulfilling them, Argentina's options were severely limited by the international situation. The cold war was in full swing, and Argentina, economically dependent on the Western bloc, could not afford a rupture in relations with the West. Every neutralist inclination was bound to be met with the determined resistance of the United States, which did not hesitate to use economic, diplomatic, and military pressure to assure that Latin America remained the most docile region within its sphere of influence.

Bending under such pressures, in 1947 Argentina joined the other Latin American nations in signing the Inter-American Treaty of Reciprocal Assistance in Rio de Janeiro (the Rio Treaty), designed to defend the hemisphere against communism. However, Argentina did not sign until it had tried to limit the treaty's scope and then delayed ratification until after the outbreak of the Korean war in 1950.[42] Meanwhile, Perón began wooing the United States, suggesting that a South American bloc under Argentine leadership would constitute the best barrier against communism and assuring that in the event of a world conflict Argentina would be allied with the United States.[43]

Argentina behaved similarly at the Bogotá conference of 1948, at which the Organization of American States (OAS) was established. Although it did join the organization, Argentina was intent on putting distance between itself and both the United States and the USSR. In response to an anticommunist resolution presented by Chile, in a speech before the conference Bramuglia replied that communism could effectively be combated only by improving Latin American living standards; he also denounced both "imperialist capitalism" and "materialist communism," and ended his speech by propagandizing the "middle way of social justice as embodied in Peronism."[44] That same year Bramuglia, in his capacity as president of the United Nations Security Council, was able to put his neutralism to good use by acting as an effective intermediary between the United States and the USSR during the Berlin crisis.

At the same time, however, Argentina was actually allying itself more and more closely with the United States against the Soviet Union. In 1948 an agreement was signed with the United States on sending a U.S. military mission to Buenos Aires,[45] and in November 1949 it closed the Slav Union—a pro-Soviet organization—during its third congress. This prompted strong protests from the Soviets, who linked the episode to a supposed "Titoist-Peronist" affinity.[46] Finally, in 1950, with the outbreak of the Korean war, Perón took an openly pro-U.S. position when he declared that Argentine troops would be part of the United Nations contingent.[47] This last proposal sparked great domestic opposition; realizing that the war would not end quickly, Perón soon reversed himself, declaring that he would act in accordance with popular wishes and that all aid would be conditional upon Argentina's receiving support from the United States in regaining sovereignty over the Islas Malvinas (Falkland Islands). In the end, he announced that he was concerned solely with the defense of the hemisphere, abandoned his promise to send troops to Korea, and limited Argentina's collaboration to the shipment of some foodstuffs.[48]

Perón's hopes that the Korean conflict would have the same beneficial effects on the Argentine economy as World War II proved to be ill founded. Beginning in 1952, the country entered a severe economic crisis, characterized by rising inflation, low foreign reserves, loss of exports, increase in the value of imports, and general recession. The bleak economic situation demonstrated the need to find new markets for exports. The first indication of rapprochement with the USSR in the area of trade came in February 1953, when Leopoldo Bravo, the new ambassador to the Soviet Union, presented his credentials. Against all expectations, Bravo was invited to meet, behind closed doors, with Stalin and Vyshinsky.[49] Shortly afterward, on 5 August 1953, both countries signed an agreement on trade and payments—the first of its type between the USSR and a Latin American country—which immediately led to a significant increase in trade (see table 2).

Trade was centered on Argentine exports of agricultural products such as hides, wool, meat, linseed oil, tannin, and so on; Soviet exports included oil, coal, iron, steel, laminated products, agricultural machinery, and equipment for the oil and railroad industries.[50] The USSR purchased 26 percent of the linseed oil exported by Argentina, 20 percent of the fine wool, and 17 percent of the hides.

The terms of the agreement called for reciprocity, granting each other the most favorable terms with respect to tariffs and customs duties, fixing prices by mutual agreement, cooperation in arriving at a balance of trade, and the prohibition of reexporting. Argentine purchases and sales were centralized in the Instituto Argentino de Promoción del Intercambio (IAPI), which had nationalized foreign trade; its Soviet counterparts were state enterprises specializing in international trade.[51]

The agreement seems to have worked out well for both parties. It is interesting to observe that at about the same time that it was being negotiated, the PCA, which up to this point had been extremely anti-Peronist, briefly toned down its hostility toward the government. A

Table 2
Argentine Trade with the Soviet Union, 1948–1970
(in thousands of U.S. dollars)

	Exports	Imports	Balance
1948	1,712	631	1,081
1949	2,105	917	1,188
1950	13	5	8
1951	6	5	1
1952	6	—	6
1953	9,293	—	9,293
1954	39,738	31,256	8,482
1955	29,735	39,067	− 9,332
1956	16,663	26,739	− 10,076
1957	14,984	4,557	9,527
1958	16,047	18,462	− 2,415
1959	20,793	22,524	− 1,731
1960	19,243	14,264	4,979
1961	14,188	13,299	889
1962	10,737	8,829	1,908
1963	15,507	3,957	11,550
1964	26,056	3,727	22,329
1965	87,057	19,401	67,656
1966	92,887	20,134	72,753
1967	26,290	7,537	18,753
1968	25,249	5,226	20,023
1969	29,478	9,116	20,362
1970	27,344	3,102	24,242

Sources: Banco Central de la República Argentina; Estremadoyro, *Relaciones ecónomicas de Argentina*, p. 78.

faction under the leadership of Juan José Real temporarily assumed control of the party and promoted an alliance with Peronism based on the possibility of nudging it in a proletarian and anti-imperialist direction. But upon their return from the Nineteenth Congress of the Communist Party of the Soviet Union (CPSU) in October 1952, Rodolfo Ghioldi and Vitorio Codovilla reassumed control of the party and succeeded in expelling Real, accusing him of "right-wing deviationism." The party reverted to a policy of confrontation with Peronism and alliance with other opposition parties. Rodolfo Puigross had also promoted conciliation with the Peronists during the early days of the government, but he never succeeded in gaining leadership of the party. Once expelled, Puigross formed a splinter group, the small Movimiento Obrero Comunista, which allied itself with the Peronists.[52]

In May 1955 an additional protocol promoting economic-commercial relations was signed, and in May-June of that year a Soviet industrial and commercial exposition was held in Buenos Aires.[53] For the first time since it had begun trading with the Soviet Union, Argentina experienced a deficit, a situation that was repeated in 1956 and again in 1958 – 59. In all three cases the deficit arose from Argentina's need to import large quantities of fuel to compensate for shortfalls in domestic production.

• Confused Times

Perón was overthrown by a coup d'etat in September 1955, and during the period of the *Revolución Libertadora* government (September 1955 – May 1958), diplomatic and commercial relations between Argentina and the Soviet Union came to an impasse. The fall in the volume of trade was more the result of Argentina's economic crisis than of the ideology of the provisional government, which harbored a conglomeration of political views ranging from anti-Peronist authoritarianism to democratic liberalism, but whose main tendencies were political antipopulism and economic neoliberalism.

Arturo Frondizi's election as president in 1958 owed much to the support given him by the proscribed Peronists. His program called for development based on the expansion of industry—especially petroleum extraction and heavy industry—and general modernization of the productive sector. The Unión Cívica Radical Intransigente (UCRI)—a branch of the Radical party headed by Frondizi—counted on the support of the PCA, which considered Frondizi a representative of the most progressive segments of the Argentine political spectrum.[54]

Frondizi, who considered foreign investment essential to the development of the Argentine economy, began to take steps almost immediately to expand commercial relations with the Soviet Union. In 1958 an agreement was signed under which the USSR would supply machinery and equipment to Argentina. Under the terms of the agreement, the USSR granted Argentina a loan of US$100 million (40 million rubles) at a low annual interest of 2 percent; the loan was to be used to purchase machinery for geological exploration and the drilling and exploitation of oil wells. The equipment to be purchased included seismological stations, drilling equipment, explosives, compressors, and transportation equipment. The loan was to be repaid in seven fixed annual quotas, and Argentina was allowed to make partial payment through exports instead of hard currency. In addition, the USSR provided Argentina with shipments of crude oil at very advantageous prices, shipments that were extremely necessary to cover the domestic production deficit. Argentine officials were pleased with the favorable terms of the loan and also by an expansion of trade that would diminish Argentina's dependence on a few countries and permit the attainment of true economic independence.[55] In May 1960 an additional protocol to the agreement was signed in which Argentina agreed to purchase road-building machinery, transportation equipment, mining equipment, and explosives, to be financed by a new Soviet loan in the amount of US$55.6 million.[56]

But Frondizi's presidency was subject to an interminable series of military "statements" expressing strong anti-Peronist and anticommunist views; these had the effect of disrupting any coherent policy, domestic or foreign.[57] This situation led to a rapid deterioration in bilateral relations and to a series of diplomatic incidents such as the expulsion in 1959 of five Soviet representatives accused of espionage and subversion;[58] a plan to reduce the number of Soviet diplomats accredited to Argentina;[59] and five attacks on the Soviet embassy between May and September 1961 during which the Argentine security forces did not intervene, provoking heated protests from Moscow.[60]

The military coup of 1962 that ousted Frondizi was followed by one of the most chaotic periods in Argentine political history; for the first time distinct factions within the armed forces engaged each other in battle, even in the streets of Buenos Aires. The only factor uniting all military factions was their antileftism, expressed in a series of vehement denunciations of communists and the Soviet Union, which led to an almost complete freezing of relations.[61] As table 2 shows, the drop in the volume of Argentine-Soviet trade was considerable, and only one-third of the additional loan issued by the Soviets was used, while entry visas were denied to the Soviet specialists who were to assist in installing equipment. Ultimately, in 1962, the Argentine government renounced the bilateral agreement on the grounds that its contractual obligations did not conform with the recently adopted policy of liberalized foreign trade. Argentina would instead subscribe to the multilateral system of trade and payments recommended by the General Agreement on Trade and Tariffs (GATT) and the International Monetary Fund (IMF).[62]

This complicated political era seemed to end when Arturo Humberto Illia, the candidate of the Unión Cívica Radical del Pueblo (UCRP), was elected president. UCRP ideology was a combination of democratic liberalism and nationalism. True to Radical tradition, Illia was in favor of nationalizing strategic industries and pursuing an independent foreign policy.[63] The Soviets were alert to the possibilities presented by the change of government and sent a special delegation to Illia's inauguration; Khruschchev himself sent a warm greeting to the new president.[64]

During 1964, 1965, and 1966, the volume of trade increased (see tables 2 and 3), accompanied by diversification of the products traded. In addition, agreement was reached on the liquidation of debts owed from the previous bilateral agreements, and negotiations began on a new commerical agreement.[65]

In its foreign policy, the Illia government adopted a moderate position with regard to the inter-American problem created by Cuba's alliance with the USSR, holding the Tricontinental Conference, and

Table 3
Soviet Trade with Argentina, 1960–1976
(in thousands of U.S. dollars)

EXPORTS

	Agricultural Products and Livestock	Nonagricultural Primary Products, Except fuels	Fuels, Lubricants, Minerals, and Related Products	Chemical Products	Manufactured Products, Chiefly Classified by Material	Transportation Equipment and Material	Miscellaneous Manufactured Products	Total[a]
1960	—	—	—	—	1,289	12,120	91	14,000
1961	—	—	—	—	510	8,281	31	10,500
1962	—	—	—	—	620	6,433	37	8,000
1963	—	9	—	—	779	49	41	900
1964	—	98	1,138	13	1,662	191	31	4,400
1965	—	33	12,430	93	4,613	205	37	20,300
1966	—	163	3,649	37	1,708	1,879	52	7,400
1967	—	—	1,721	48	1,413	1,579	18	4,800
1968	—	—	355	—	2,305	528	58	3,200
1969	4,497	—	45	381	1,325	439	85	6,800
1970	—	—	201	398	658	268	25	1,900
1971	—	—	205	472	967	374	33	2,100
1972	—	—	77	1,037	492	458	14	2,200
1973	—	—	—	1,551	1,088	3,368	51	6,100
1974	—	—	—	3,565	1,608	1,931	87	7,900
1975	—	—	—	1,190	1,477	11,159	50	14,800
1976	—	—	—	3,334	—	8,156	194	11,800

IMPORTS

1960	—	17,514	2,565	447	—	12	21,700
1961	—	13,467	6,340	—	—	11	19,900
1962	—	9,734	—	142	—	30	9,800
1963	748	13,152	4,060	—	—	6	18,400
1964	8,911	6,266	4,433	—	—	11	19,900
1965	42,175	20,580	8,933	—	—	8	72,000
1966	79,837	23,752	3,740	—	—	10	107,300
1967	1,128	19,060	1,593	660	—	14	23,100
1968	1,612	23,730	662	2,309	—	8	28,700
1969	8,002	14,835	557	1,311	800	26	25,500
1970	—	23,459	7,901	—	—	31	31,300
1971	12,098	15,837	5,481	—	—	38	33,800
1972	—	14,966	4,392	—	4,936	8	27,600
1973	3,208	64,710	—	—	15,045	7	97,900
1974	100,394	48,951	13	—	16,512	13	173,600
1975	331,173	40,160	5,964	—	17,727	482	407,200
1976	217,473	36,172	12,941	—	35,319	32	312,500
	1,550						

Source: Evgueni Kossarev, Relaciones económicas entre los países de América Latina y los países miembros del CAME (Santiago: E/CEPAL/PROY. 4/R.16, 1979).

a. Totals exceed sum of yearly figures because only the most important items are enumerated in the table. These figures may differ from those presented in table 2 and 4 because they were calculated by converting from rubles to dollars based on the rates of exchange presented in the UN *Yearbook of International Trade Statistics*.

creation of the Organization of Latin American Solidarity (OLAS). After some vacillation, Argentina refused to commit troops to the inter-American force sent to the Dominican Republic. Although this defiance of the United States earned it the good will of the USSR and Cuba, it was also an important cause of discontent among the military and helped unleash the coup of 1966.

• The *Revolución Argentina* and Ideological Frontiers

The coup d'etat of June 1966 ironically placed General Juan C. Onganía, a former opponent of military intervention in politics, in the presidency. Among the first actions were the dissolution of Congress and the political parties and the imposition of a political system combining authoritarian corporatism in the political sphere with orthodox liberalism in the economic. An immediate indication of the profoundly anticommunist character of the new government was the promulgation of the Statute of Basic Acts of the Argentine Revolution (the name the new military government gave itself), which singled out Marxism as one of the principal causes of Argentina's problems.[66] Hardline anti-communist policy was given concrete expression in the 1967 Law of Defense Against Communism, the language of which was broad enough to cover practically the whole of the Argentine left and even part of the Peronist opposition.[67]

At the same time, a number of anti-Soviet incidents occurred, contributing to a total freezing of relations between the two countries. The first incidents involved the illegal presence of Soviet fishing vessels in waters claimed by Argentina, against which the military government lodged strong protests with the USSR. In addition, General Onganía announced that his foreign policy was to be based on "ideological frontiers," an extension of national security policy. Claiming that international communism had made the concept of territorial frontiers obsolete and that distinctions between domestic and foreign enemies were no longer relevant, Onganía embarked on a program of extermination of internal "subversives" and open confrontation with the communist and procommunist countries.[68]

The first major incident between Argentina and the Soviet Union occurred in 1967 when a group of Argentine officials attempted to inspect the contents of Soviet diplomatic correspondence located on board the ship *Michurinsk* anchored in the port of Buenos Aires. The captain's refusal to permit the inspection led to a scuffle between Soviet sailors and Argentine officials, producing some bruises and an exchange of protests between the foreign offices of both countries.[69]

In August 1968 the Argentine government strongly condemned the Soviet invasion of Czechoslovakia, stating that it "seriously affects world peace and is clear evidence of the disregard for the principles of coexistence between states." The government also offered its full support to any action recommended by the Security Council of the United Nations for restoring normal conditions in Czechoslovakia.[70]

The most serious incident occurred in March 1970 when a group of extreme rightists headed by an official of the Policía Federal Argentina attempted to kidnap the commercial attaché of the Soviet embassy, Yuri Pirovarov. The last-minute intervention of another member of the Argentine security forces prevented the kidnappers from carrying out their plan, but the incident significantly increased tensions between the two countries.[71] Later, in June 1970, two Soviet diplomats were arrested during a "political" meeting, and the government expelled them for having engaged in "activities incompatible with their diplomatic functions."[72]

A few days after this incident, conflicts within the armed forces over how to handle the explosive Argentine political situation led to General Onganía's removal from the presidency and his replacement, after a short interregnum exercised by the joint chiefs of staff, by General Roberto M. Levingston on 18 June 1970.[73]

It can safely be said the Onganía presidency represented one of the lowest points in the history of Argentine-Soviet relations, as witnessed by the incidents mentioned above and by the drop in volume of trade. The 1970s opened in a climate of estrangement and hostility, but against all expectations, relations between Argentina and the Soviet Union were to emerge in the course of the decade as among the most interesting phenomena in contemporary Latin American international relations.

2 The Endless Spiral: Economic Ties since 1970

- The Military Government and the Collapse
  of Ideological Frontiers

The 1970s were years of such volatile and contradictory changes in Argentine politics, society, and economics that it would be premature to say the final chapter has been written on that period. The changes, conflicts, and tumults of those years continue to affect present-day Argentina and will continue to affect the country's evolution for a long time to come.

As the decade opened, it was increasingly apparent that the "Argentine Revolution" and the model of development it sought to impose on the country had failed completely. The country was wracked by acute political conflicts (urban revolts, guerrilla activities, government repression) and grave economic problems (recession, inflation, disruption of foreign trade). General Levingston's answer to the nation's difficulties was to revitalize the nationalist-authoritarian model initiated in 1966, but he was opposed first by the civilian sector and then by his comrades in the armed forces, who soon removed him from power. His brief period in office (June 1970–March 1971) was a continuation of the so-called hegemonic stalemate among Argentine socioeconomic sectors, whose conflicting interests guaranteed that any coherent policies would soon fall apart at the seams.[1]

Under these circumstances, Argentine-Soviet trade relations continued to be adversely affected, hobbling along at the low level to which they had descended in the Onganía era. However, there was slight evidence of an easing in tensions in that no new diplomatic incidents occurred and the volume of trade increased marginally during 1971 (see tables 2 and 3).

The improvement in the volume of trade had little to do with

Levingston or the agreements signed during his administration, even though the presence in the cabinet of ministers like Aldo Ferrer (economics) might have led to a more aggressive trade policy in search of new markets. The political and economic situation continued to deteriorate steadily, culminating in the second *Cordobazo* or *Viborazo* in Córdoba in early March 1971, a violent labor and student uprising that led to Levingston's ouster by his military colleagues.

The ascension to the presidency of the army commander in chief, General Alejandro A. Lanusse, the true "strong man" of the armed forces, resulted in a number of changes in the Argentine political scene.

Confronted with a popular revolt, the military sought a solution to the country's problems by negotiating with the largest political groups, the Peronists and the Radicals. Both Onganía and Levingston had given top priority to economic development in the hope that prosperity would provide a natural solution to political problems, but politics as such now came to dominate the national agenda. The Lanusse government tried to implement what it called the "Grand National Accord," a political pact that would guarantee the survival of existing socioeconomic structures in return for the military's orderly retirement to the barracks and the holding of general elections in which, for the first time since 1955, the Peronists would be allowed to participate openly. Although Lanusse was ultimately unsuccessful in his attempt to neutralize the power of Peronism by tying it down in alliances, he did succeed in protecting the nation's socioeconomic structure from revolutionary change. He also maintained the unity of the army, keeping intact its future options despite the strategic retreat forced on it by the Peronist victory in the 1973 elections.[2]

The Lanusse government also differed radically from its predecessors in foreign policy. First of all, it declared an end to the policy of "ideological frontiers," which had in effect amounted to a refusal to develop relations with socialist, reformist, or revolutionary governments. The new catchword in Argentine foreign policy was "ideological pluralism."

The first indication of Argentina's new flexibility was a series of meetings between Lanusse and Salvador Allende in 1971. The two presidents agreed to open negotiations on the Beagle Channel dispute, and Argentina extended Chile a line of credit for the purchase of Argentine products. The Argentine government also used these meetings to proclaim publicly its new orientation in foreign policy.[3] At the same time, Argentina established friendly relations with the reformist governments of Peru and Bolivia; forged closer ties with the democratic governments of Colombia, Ecuador, Mexico, and Venezuela; and dissociated itself from the military government in Brazil. In February 1972 diplomatic relations were established, and ambassadors exchanged, with the People's Republic of China.

The first economic consequences of this diplomatic shift were large increases in Argentine exports to Chile, which increased from US$91 million in 1970 to US$129 million in 1971, US$163 million in 1972, and US$233 million in 1973, providing Argentina with favorable trade balances of US$16, $60, $107, and $151 million, respectively.[4]

As far as the USSR was concerned, talks concerning the implementation of the trade agreement initiated by the Illia government in 1965 and abandoned by Onganía after the 1966 coup were quickly reopened. The new contacts proved fruitful, and on 25 June 1971 a final agreement was signed in Moscow, to take effect on 30 May 1972.[5] This trade agreement was signed with the "desire of promoting economic relations and expanding trade between both countries on the basis of mutual advantage." It included the following points:

a. The contracting parties would grant each other the maximum possible trading facilities (article 1).
b. They would accord each other most-favored-nation status (article 2), which implied favored treatment of each other's ships in port (article 3).
c. They would prohibit reexports except in cases of previous agreement (article 5).
d. They would strive to expand the proportion of manufactured products within the total volume of trade (article 7).
e. They would pay for purchases in freely convertible currencies (article 8).
f. The agreement would be valid for three years from the date of signing and would be automatically renewed unless notification

to the contrary was given sixty days prior to its expiration (article 12).[6]

From the Soviet point of view, the most favorable aspect of the agreement was acquiring most-favored-nation status. Most countries with market or mixed economies refused to grant this status to the USSR because it practiced a foreign trade monopoly and did not belong to GATT, unlike other socialist countries such as Hungary, Poland, Rumania, and Czechoslovakia.[7]

From the Argentine point of view, the most important aspects of the agreement were the obligation on both sides to pay in freely convertible currency[8] and the mutual promise to increase the volume of trade in manufactured and semimanufactured products.

Although the agreement represented a great improvement in the tone of bilateral relations, its practical effects were more modest. In fact, due to the economic and political difficulties facing Argentina, the total volume of exports to the USSR in 1972 fell to US$24 million, while Soviet imports entering Argentina declined to US$2.6 million.

Nevertheless, the Lanusse government was an important period in the history of Argentine-Soviet relations because it laid the foundation for the rapid development of relations after 1972. The easing of diplomatic and political tensions was important in and of itself. In contrast to past experience, and especially the anti-Soviet feeling during Onganía's presidency, relations began to develop on a pragmatic basis of mutual economic convenience. Both countries chose to ignore political and ideological differences and refrained from issuing hostile declarations, exchanging diplomatic notes, or expelling diplomats. Conflicts were limited to incursions of Soviet fishing vessels in Argentine waters, but even these incidents were settled with greater discretion than previously.

Even more important than the easing in diplomatic tensions and signing of trade agreements was the fact that the initiatives came from an Argentine military government. In a country as politically unstable as Argentina, where civilian governments are constantly threatened by a coup-prone military, anticommunism and anti-Sovietism have been effective weapons in preparing a climate favorable to military intervention. As a result, civilian governments have always acted with extreme caution in their dealings with the USSR. That a military government took the initiative in improving relations with the USSR was both a novelty and an assurance that the old arguments against ties with the Soviet Union would be less threatening to future governments, civilian or military.

• Peronism and the Opening to the East

The Argentine general elections of March 1973 resulted in a large plurality for the united front of the Peronists and their minor allies. On 25 May 1973 Hector J. Cámpora was inaugurated as president. His extremely brief term of office—May–July 1973—was marked by intense conflict within the governing party and by political and social unrest at the national level. In July 1973 Cámpora resigned in order to permit the holding of new elections in which Juan D. Perón could participate (he had been prevented from taking part in the March elections). The fall of Cámpora, instigated by the trade unions and the Peronist right, suggested that the period of mass radicalization, which had peaked in early 1973, was beginning to ebb. For the first time since 1955, the military and the decidedly anti-Peronist conservatives considered Perón the lesser evil, a viable alternative for containing the process of mass radicalization, and thus they did not oppose his return to power. New elections were held during the interregnum of Raúl Lastiri, the president of the Chamber of Deputies and an antileftist Peronist. The Peronist ticket won by a large majority, and Perón and his wife, María E. Martínez (Isabel) de Perón, took office as president and vice-president in October 1973.[9]

Despite the rapid and often profound changes that occurred in this period—from March 1973 until shortly after the death of Perón in July 1974—Argentine-Soviet relations grew steadily more cordial. The reasons for improved relations were at once political, ideological, and economic, and related to the kind of public policies that the Peronist government tried to implement.

The Peronists returned to power perhaps even more devoted than they had been eighteen years before to the doctrine of the "Third Position," which called for neutrality vis-à-vis the USSR and the United States and the maintenance of friendly relations with all states. Adherence to the "Third Position" was reinforced by the fact that in the years since 1955 the nonaligned nations of the Third World had increased in numbers and formed organizations able to exercise effective influence on world affairs. This new international situation naturally led the Peronists to propose a foreign policy that would diminish Argentina's dependence on the advanced capitalist countries by establishing new and deeper ties with the socialist countries and the Third World. The Argentine shift toward nonalignment was welcomed by the Soviets, who regarded it as a "Latin American step" on the way toward "the second stage of the national liberation movement: the struggle to eliminate economic backwardness and the struggle against feudal and capitalist relations of exploitation," which would proceed from anti-imperialism to anti-capitalism and ultimately to the building of a socialist society.[10]

An economic factor that must have weighed heavily in the Peronist decision to initiate an opening to the East was the ever increasing difficulty Argentina faced in selling its exports in traditional markets. The EEC countries had erected trade barriers to protect their own agricultural producers, and by 1974–75 the Common Market was virtually closed to Argentine agricultural products. This situation was aggravated by the oil crisis of 1973, which restricted the purchase of Argentine exports in other important markets of Latin America and the Third World. All this reinforced the Argentine determination to find new markets, and the most obvious alternatives were the communist countries, especially the USSR, which had a continuing need for meat and grain and was less affected by the energy crisis.

The Peronist government had ambitious plans for industrial development, and the Soviet Union was regarded as a potential alternative supplier of capital goods and advanced technology whose attractive payment and financing terms could reduce Argentina's technological dependence on the developed countries of the West.

But the most important factor in expanding relations with the USSR was the presence in the cabinet of José B. Gelbard, the minister of economics from May 1973 to October 1974, whose decisions concerning national and international economic policy probably outweighed all the influences mentioned above. Gelbard was an old ally of the Peronist movement; as early as 1952 he had headed the Confederación General Económica (GGE), a business organization created with the support of Perón to counteract the influence of the traditional, anti-Peronist business associations. Its initial nucleus consisted of small- and medium-sized businesses, especially in the interior of the country. As a Peronist organization, the CGE was disbanded after the 1955 coup, but it was later resurrected, seeing its ranks swell as the possibility of Perón's return to power became more likely. During this period, Gelbard's own economic power increased considerably, and his group of businesses came to include some of the most important in the Argentine market, including FATE (tires and electronics), ALUAR (aluminum), BGH (household appliances), and a number of financial institutions.

When Gelbard became minister of economics in May 1973, he adopted, with Perón's wholehearted support, a relatively autonomous development strategy based on an alliance among business, labor, and the state (the so-called Social Pact), which included the establishment of protectionist measures against foreign capital, the creation of conditions for the intensive exploitation of agriculture, the nationalization of bank deposits, the gradual redistribution of income in favor of wage earners, and the opening of new foreign markets.[11]

What most concerns us here is the opening of new foreign markets for traditional and nontraditional Argentine exports.[12] Once in office, the Peronist government quickly proceeded to develop closer relations with the socialist countries and established diplomatic relations with Cuba, the German Democratic Republic, North Vietnam, and North Korea. Even more important was the visit to Cuba of the "Gelbard Mission," the first significant break in the economic embargo of Cuba since the Punta del Este conference in 1963.[13] Cuba was extended credit in the amount of US$200 million annually for six years, for a total of US$1.2 billion, to be used to purchase Argentine automobiles, trucks, tractors, agricultural machinery, and other products.[14]

The Peronist government also acted quickly to improve relations with the Soviet Union. In June 1973 the Argentine-Soviet chamber of commerce was created, consisting of commercial, industrial, agricultural, financial, tourist, and transportation institutions and enterprises, public and private, from both countries. It is one of the few organizations of its type in the Western world.[15] The essential function of the chamber, which has eighty Argentine members, is to establish contacts between buyers and sellers in both countries in order to increase the flow of trade.

In February 1974 a Soviet delegation headed by Alexei N. Manzhulo, vice-minister of foreign trade for the USSR, visited Argentina. After a series of negotiations, Manzhulo signed an agreement with the Argentine minister of foreign relations, Alberto J. Vignes, aimed at developing economic-commercial and scientific-technical cooperation.[16] According to the agreement, both countries were "animated by the desire to strengthen and develop economic-commercial and scientific-technical cooperation, as well as cooperation in the field of maritime navigation" and desired to promote and diversify this cooperation upon the basis of "respect for sovereignty, national independence, nonintervention in the internal affairs of all other countries, equality of rights, and mutual benefits." More specifically, both countries agreed:

a. to cooperate economically, commercially, scientifically, and technically in the development of each other's economies, especially in the fields of metallurgy, oil, gas, iron, coal, cellulose, refrigeration, pharmaceuticals, petrochemicals, coal-based chemicals, road-building, communications, electrical and nuclear energy, shipbuilding, fishing, and agriculture (article 1);
b. that cooperation would be implemented through increased trade, coparticipation in the construction of industrial plants, exchange of licenses, patents, know-how, and information, visits by scientific delegations, and the joint study of economic problems (article 2);
c. that cooperation would extend to the field of maritime navigation (article 4);
d. that relations would be strengthened by facilitating the freedom of movement of each other's officials and that the results of the cooperation developed as a result of the agreement would not be retransmitted to third parties (articles 5 and 6);
e. that the agreement would be provisionally in force pending its

ratification by both countries,[17] would remain in force for a period of ten years, and would be automatically renewable for periods of one year unless previous notice to the contrary was given (article 8).

A new agreement on the supply of Soviet machinery and equipment to Argentina was also signed during this Soviet visit as a complement to the trade agreement of 1971.[18] The agreement would be in force for five years and provided not only for the purchase of Soviet equipment, but also for surveying and installation. The financial conditions of the agreement were very favorable to Argentina, establishing a system of payments deferrable up to ten years, with an annual interest rate of 4.5 percent for state-owned Argentine enterprises and 5 percent for privately owned companies. The agreement also provided that the USSR would use the income earned from these sales to import Argentine products, 30 percent of which were to be manufactured or semi-manufactured products bought at normal market prices.[19]

An agreement on scientific-technical cooperation was signed on the same occasion. It provided for the exchange of professional experts and scientific-technical information, scholarships, joint congresses and symposia, the development of technological processes for agriculture and industry, and carrying out joint projects according to contract.[20]

On 22 April 1974 the Soviet firm Energomashexport won an international bid for supplying twelve 135-megawatt turbines for the Salto Grande hydroelectric power plant located on the Uruguay River, at a total value of US$170 million. The Salto Grande plant is a joint Argentine-Uruguayan project for which Argentina bears most of the cost. This was the first time a Soviet firm had entered an international bidding competition; it competed against firms from six other countries and accepted regulations based on Western technology. Later the Soviet Union contracted to supply two more turbines. The Soviet offer was approximately 30 percent lower than that of its closest competitor; its financing conditions included a ten-year loan at 4 percent annual interest, 5 percent amortization to the contracting firm and another 5 percent upon delivery, with a grace period for payment until installation and construction were completed, and a loan of US$10 million to assist in the installation of the machinery. The project is partially financed by the Inter-American Development Bank and the World Bank, and this is the first case where Western financial organizations have cooperated with Soviet sources on the same project. The final agreement on terms of payment for the machinery also provided that Argentine and Uruguayan exports could be used for partial payment in a proportion of 70 percent and 30 percent, respectively.[21]

The Soviet Union's successful bid led to the establishment in 1974 of the first Argentine-Soviet industrial venture, a joint enterprise formed by the firms Ingeniería Tauro and Energomashexport to supply material for the installation of the hydroelectric equipment.

In May 1974 Gelbard, accompanied by a delegation of 135 Argentine officials, visited Eastern Europe and signed a number of trade agreements with the USSR, Poland, Hungary, and Czechoslovakia. During his stay in the Soviet Union (3–8 May), Gelbard and his retinue were greeted with unusual cordiality by high-level Soviet officials, and the minister met at length in private sessions with the secretary general of the CPSU, Leonid Brezhnev; the president of the Presidium of the Supreme Soviet of the USSR, Nikolai Podgorny; and the president of the Soviet Council of Ministers, Alexei Kosygin. Gelbard reported that the three leaders had "a great interest in Argentina and show[ed] true understanding of its problems." He emphasized that they "had expressed great enthusiasm for a visit by Perón" during 1974, and concluded by saying that his visit opened "a new page in the relations between the two countries."[22] *Pravda* observed, "At this moment relations [between Argentina and the USSR] are taking on more concrete shape and entering a new stage."[23]

During his visit Gelbard discussed a number of agreements, among them the possibility of the USSR's granting a loan of US$600 million to be used for the purchase of hydroelectric equipment for the Salto Grande and Alicura stations, the expansion of the Chocón plant, and the construction of thermal power stations. At the same time, a number of commercial agreements were signed, which included a Soviet promise to purchase from Argentina 100,000 tons of meat, 100,000 tons of corn, fresh fruits and concentrated juices, shoes, chemical products, and wines.[24]

The negotiations also touched on the possibility of Soviet cooperation in such large-scale projects as the harnessing of the Middle Paraná, the construction of thermoelectric plants, extension of high-voltage lines, construction of a laminated metals plant, exploitation of coal mines, and the establishment of a lignite concentrator and oil refineries.[25] Negotiators also discussed the possibility of establishing regularly scheduled flights between Moscow and Buenos Aires by Aerolíneas Argentinas and Aeroflot, a project in which the Soviets were especially interested.

On 7 May 1974 a protocol was signed creating the Argentine-Soviet joint commission on economic-commercial and scientific-technical cooperation; it held its first meeting in Moscow in September 1974.[26] The joint commission played an important role in consolidating and expanding bilateral ties by permitting the exchange of information, coordination of activities, and controlling the pace of agreements and accords. It was most effective as a mechanism guaranteeing the continuity of relations, but was weakened by the fact that its members lacked the authority to sign agreements, accords, and contracts.

Although such negotiations were important in setting the stage for the expansion of trade, they were often merely an expression of good intentions antedating any concrete realities. A major problem was securing ratification of the agreements in the first place. Although Soviet ratification was virtually automatic, Argentine ratification tended to be delayed, especially when the political or economic situation changed after their signing. In a report on Latin American relations with the socialist countries, the Economic Commission for Latin America (ECLA) has pointed out that often "one gets the impression that in discussions concerning projects of cooperation no selective criterion is applied; instead, the intention is to include the greatest number of fields or sectors possible, leaving it to later negotiations to determine what is practicable or viable . . . ; accordingly, the difference between the number of projects agreed on or planned and the number that actually reach the stage of execution is relatively large."[27]

The plan to increase the volume of trade was hampered by a number of other problems, including agreements Argentine exporters had already signed with other purchasers, the absence of permanent trade representatives, the lack of information on Soviet equipment and technology—often considered inferior to Western technology—the Soviets' disinclination to participate in international bids, the problem of maintaining equipment with which Argentine technicians were unfamiliar, and the lack of maintenance service by the Soviets. On the Argentine side, constant shifts in government economic and investment policy and the deepening economic and political crisis often led to delays in installing equipment or simple abandonment of the projects.[28]

As a result, many of the specific agreements signed in Moscow were never carried out. The value of Argentine exports to Russia stabilized or increased slightly, but only for traditional products such as wheat, corn, wool, hides, and meat. But these increases were not in the amounts foreseen, and there was no increase in the importance of manufactured products.

Expansion of Soviet exports to Argentina was negligible, increasing from US$6.1 million in 1973 to US$7.9 million in 1974. Even though their value doubled to US$14.8 million in 1975, they still represented an extremely insignificant proportion of total Argentine imports, which amounted to US$2.229 billion, $3.636 billion, and $3.947 billion, respectively, for the years 1973, 1974, and 1975. The Soviet Union's only success in establishing a solid base for placing its products in Argentina was in the field of electric energy production. In 1974, in addition to winning the bid for the Salto Grande turbines, it also succeeded in reaching an agreement to supply three 310-megawatt thermoelectric plants to be installed at San Nicolás (Buenos Aires Province), Luján de Cuyo (Mendoza), and the SEGBA VII power plant (Buenos Aires).

However, a number of problems soon developed. During the bidding process, Energomashexport had promised to use international technical standards in constructing the turbines for Salto Grande, but the Soviet manufacturer refused to honor the commitment made by the negotiating firm. This led to a number of difficulties because the MEIN firm—an international consortium of Argentine, Uruguayan, and U.S. companies charged with supervision of the project—wanted to guarantee that the Soviets were employing international standards. The Soviets appeared to be using their own standards, adapted from old German guidelines. Only after difficult negotiations did the consulting firm's technicians succeed in visiting the Soviet Union and assuring that the work was performed according to the desired guidelines, but the difficulties in gaining access to the manufacturers and making frequent inspections continued.[29]

Problems developed on the Argentine-Uruguayan side when installation began because the contract stipulated that only sixteen Soviet technicians could be at the construction site at one time, which led to protests from the technicians supervising the work.[30] The principal problem with the thermoelectric plants was repeated delays on the part of the Argentine contracting firm. The contract was eventually renegotiated in 1976, and the site of the plants was changed from San Nicolás and Luján de Cuyo to Bahía Blanca.[31]

Despite these problems, both countries continued to intensify and diversify bilateral contacts during 1974. In July 1974, 12,000 tons of meat valued at US$15 million were sold to the Soviet Union, in addition to a previously negotiated sale worth US$10 million, helping to ease the difficulties created by the imminent closing of the Common Market to meat imports in October of that year.[32]

In August 1974 an agreement on maritime transportation was signed in Buenos Aires in which both countries specified the facilities they would grant each other with respect to most-favored-nation status for each other's ships and the use of port facilities.[33]

About the same time, talks were opened to establish joint studies south of the forty-second parallel in Argentine territory and organize a training center with Soviet instructors to train specialists for the fishing industry. The possibility of building a new fishing port in Argentina (Punta Quilla) was also discussed, as well as the probable constitution of a joint Argentine-Soviet enterprise.

In September 1974 a Soviet commercial exposition of equipment and machinery was held in Buenos Aires, during which equipment valued at US$6.6 million was placed in the Argentine market.[34] The joint commission also held its first meeting in Moscow that month and discussed the possibility of cooperation in the fields of energy, metallurgy, fishing, and science and technology, as well as the expansion of trade between the two countries.[35] The meeting culminated in the signing of an agreement under the terms of which Argentina agreed to sell the Soviet Union 100,000 tons of meat and 500,000 hectoliters of wine between 1974 and 1977. Further negotiations were planned to determine the quality of the products and the means of shipment.[36] In October 1974 an agreement was signed for the Soviet purchase of 300,000 tons of corn between April and June 1975.[37] This last purchase was in addition to 150,000 tons of the same product scheduled to be delivered in November-December 1974; total Soviet purchases were approaching a minimum of 900,000 tons.[38]

• The Crisis of Peronism and the Deterioration of Relations

While these agreements were being worked out, the Argentine domestic situation had undergone considerable change. Juan Perón died on 1 July 1974 and was succeeded in the presidency by his wife and running mate, María E. Martínez de Perón. The death of the leader who for thirty years had profoundly influenced the political, social, and economic configuration of contemporary Argentina led to rapid changes in all aspects of national life. His disappearance from the political arena removed the principal element of cohesion in the Peronist movement and left the door open to a violent crisis that ended in the military coup of 1976.

Isabel Perón's government initiated a number of policy shifts, largely at the instigation of José López Rega, the minister of social welfare. A bizarre figure who combined mystical and fascistoid inclinations with an insatiable lust for power, López Rega became the president's most influential adviser. At the same time, the Peronist trade union leaders and leading officials of the Justicialist party also increased their power. This situation resulted in a series of conflicts within the cabinet, culminating in the removal of Gelbard from the economics ministry under the pressure of the *Lopezreguista,* union, and party factions.[39] With the initial support of this coalition, Alfredo Gómez Morales, an economist with a long career in the Peronist movement who had directed the stabilization program in 1952, became minister of economics. He quickly moved to imprint his more orthodox policies on the economy by trying to control government spending, restricting the money supply, and readjusting price levels and fees for public services.

Gómez Morales's policies succeeded in pleasing no one, and in June 1975 he was supplanted by López Rega's candidate, Celestino Rodrigo, who subjected the economy to shock treatment (devaluation of the peso by 100 percent, a 175 percent increase in the price of gasoline, a 75 percent increase in the price of electricity, and total abolition of price controls). At the same time, the government attempted to impose wage control by decree, provoking the first general strike called by the CGT against a Peronist government. In yet another shift within the governing party, the trade unions gained the upper hand and ousted the *Lopezreguistas* from positions of power. Rodrigo was replaced as minister of economics by Antonio Cafiero, the CGT's candidate. But the crisis was by now out of control, affecting every aspect of national life. The Peronist bloc in both houses of Congress split into factions supporting and opposing the president; a similar division occurred within the trade unions. The commander in chief of the army, Numa Laplane, who was opposed to a military coup, was replaced by General Jorge Videla in an internal putsch. The struggle between the armed forces and the guerrillas was becoming increasingly violent on both sides. The economy had entered a critical period, characterized by rocketing inflation (350 percent in 1975), shortages, strikes, lockouts, declining gross national product (minus 2 percent in 1975) and investment (minus 16 percent), and a huge balance-of-payments deficit with a corresponding loss of foreign currency reserves. The government proved incapable of providing any solution to this catastrophe, despite successive reshufflings of the cabinet in the final months before it was overthrown by a military coup on 24 March 1976.

As the Argentine political scene grew ever more chaotic, relations with the Soviet Union entered a gradual impasse from which they emerged only after the 1976 coup. Some conservative groups had been opposed all along to Gelbard's economic policy because they considered closer contacts with the socialist countries a threat to national security and were fearful of the country's becoming dependent on the Soviet bloc.[40] Such views found resonance in Isabel Perón's government, whose foreign policy, though muddled, appeared to give priority to relations with the Third World (especially the Arab countries, which were regarded as a potential source of loans and investment), Western

Europe, and the United States. Furthermore, the rapid deterioration of the economic and political situation reduced the amount of exportable commodities and foreign reserves that could have been used to increase exports to the USSR and imports from it.

Bilateral relations quickly came to a standstill after the fall of Gelbard: previously signed agreements went unratified, meetings of the joint commission were suspended, and no new agreements of comparable importance and diversity as those of the previous period were signed.

The only important economic development during this period was the visit by a Soviet commercial delegation in 1975, which signed contracts for the purchase of wool, hides, quebracho extract, wine, and cane syrup. Argentina agreed to the purchase of two stubbers, mining explosives and ventilators, and a lamination train for the fabrication of tubes. In addition, preliminary agreement was reached on the sale of equipment for manufacturing cotton yarn and of sixty trackless trolleys for the city of Rosario.[41]

In July 1975 an agreement was signed between Agua y Energía Eléctrica de Argentina and the Soviet firm Technopromexport; the Soviet firm contracted to provide assistance in the exploration and design of a hydroelectric complex on the Middle Paraná. The USSR agreed to provide the exploration equipment and specialists to carry out the study at an approximate cost of US$8 million, to be paid over ten years at 4.5 percent annual interest. The Middle Paraná is a 600-kilometer-long branch of the Paraná River between Paso de la Patria (Corrientes Province) in the north and the imaginary line joining the cities of Paraná and Santa Fé in the south. Argentina plans to construct hydroelectric power plants with a total capacity of 5.3 million kilowatts generating 3.2 billion kilowatt-hours per year on the river.[42] The project is extremely complex and includes two dams, Chapetón in the south and Machuca-Cue (Pati) in the north. In addition to harnessing the river for electricity generation, these dams will also improve navigability, provide irrigation, offer flood protection, and facilitate the construction of roads in their vicinity. Total investment for the construction of the project was estimated to be approximately US$4.2 billion (in 1975 dollars). It was also estimated that eight years would be required to complete the project once construction began. However, Argentina failed to ratify the contract, and only after a series of delays was it renegotiated and approved in 1978.[43]

Despite these difficulties, the contracts signed during Gelbard's tenure assured that trade with the Soviet Union, and specifically Argentine exports, continued at a high level. However, the only important contract signed by the two countries in the period after Gelbard's fall was a Soviet agreement, in September 1975, to purchase one million tons of grain (250,000 tons of corn and sorghum and 750,000 tons of wheat). This transaction was a matter of necessity to both countries: the Soviet Union needed to cover a temporary shortage occasioned by a U.S. prohibition of grain exports, while Argentina desperately required foreign exchange to ease its balance-of-payments problems.[44]

A survey of Argentine-Soviet trade during the second Peronist era (1973–1976) reveals some important patterns (see table 4). The export of Argentine products to the USSR had grown gradually, from US$85.1 million in 1973 to US$211.1 million in 1974, US$288.3 million in 1975, only to drop to US$219.1 million in 1976. Soviet exports to Argentina, although much lower in absolute value, paralleled this growth, increas-

Table 4
Argentine Trade with the Soviet Union, 1971–1981
(in thousands of U.S. dollars)

	Exports	*Imports*	*Balance (+)*
1971	30,348	3,882	26,466
1972	24,101	2,601	21,500
1973	85,091	7,010	78,081
1974	211,145	10,911	200,234
1975	288,314	21,941	266,373
1976	219,118	12,784	206,334
1977	211,000	20,300	190,700
1978	385,000	11,100	373,900
1979	418,620	35,960	382,660
1980	1,685,050	44,080	1,640,970
1981[a]	3,439,400	44,950	3,394,450

Source: Banco Central de la República Argentina; Instituto Nacional de Estadísticas y Censos.

a. Estimated figures.

ing from US$7 million in 1973 to US$10.9 million in 1974, US$21.9 million in 1975, and falling to US$12.8 million in 1976.

The largest share of Argentine exports consisted of primary products such as wheat, corn, sorghum, wool, and meat; simply processed products such as tanned hides and wine; and, of far less importance, manufactured products such as yarns, metal tubing, shoes, and books. The majority of Soviet exports were manufactured products: machinery, transportation equipment and vehicles, explosives, storage tanks, bearings, trucks, pharmaceuticals, and books. The only semiprocessed exports were chemicals such as bichromate of soda or metals such as cast iron.

Analysis of these statistics reveals that Argentine-Soviet trade retained its traditional pattern despite increased volume. The Soviet Union continued to experience a high trade deficit: US$76.1 million in 1973, US$200.2 million in 1974, US$266.4 million in 1975, decreasing to US$206.3 million in 1976. Agrentina continued to export traditional agricultural products without any significant increase in the proportion of manufactured or semi-manufactured goods.

This situation was a cause of concern to both countries, if for different reasons. Soviet experts expressed dissatisfaction with their country's trade deficit and hoped that a certain equilibrium in the volume of trade could eventually be reached, emphasizing that the complementarity of both countries' productive sectors could lead the way to a more stable and planned division of labor.[45] Argentine experts, on the other hand, insisted on the necessity of diversifying Argentine exports to include a greater proportion of manufactured goods. This was considered essential if the country were to avoid the vulnerability it had experienced as an exclusive exporter of primary products.[46]

• The Military Government and the Expansion of Economic Relations

The coup d'etat of 24 March 1976 that placed General Jorge R. Videla in the presidency led to a number of important changes in domestic economic policy. After a period of readjustment, relations with the USSR began to expand.

The new economic team headed by Minister José A. Martínez de Hoz instituted a program whose fundamental objectives were eliminating inflation, removing the danger of default, accelerating the rate of economic growth, and ending conflicts between capital and labor.[47] To achieve these objectives, the government adopted an orthodox liberal economic strategy which sought to open the economy to the foreign competition and investment and unleash market forces (with the exception of labor). The Martínez de Hoz program aimed to totally revamp the existing economic structure, which has been variously described as statist, interventionist, and protectionist. At least two conditions had to be met in order for this plan to succeed: (1) holding down inflation by freezing wages and (2) improving the balance of payments by expanding the volume of exports and by attracting investment and loans from abroad.[48]

The necessity of improving the balance of payments partially explains why a military government engaged in harsh repression of armed insurgency and most of the Argentine left—in the name of "Western and Christian civilization"—refrained from publicly denouncing communism and the socialist countries as the instigators of the domestic crisis, which had been the practice of military governments since 1930. In any case, the government did not freeze relations with the USSR. Given Argentina's difficulties in placing its exports in the world market, it was obvious, even to a military government, that closing the door to economic relations with the socialist countries, and especially the Soviet Union, would only make a bad situation worse. Accordingly, Videla's government continued to honor trade agreements signed by its predecessors and began anew the intensification of relations that had faltered toward the end of the Peronist era.

In July 1976 the contract between Energomashexport and Agua y Energía Eléctrica and SEGBA for the supply of three turbogenerators for the power plants at Bahía Blanca and the Central Costanera plant in Buenos Aires, abandoned during the previous period, was renegotiated and ratified. In November 1976 the Argentine-Soviet joint commission, which had been suspended in 1975, held its second meeting in Argentina. At this meeting the commission studied the possibilities of increasing trade and pointed out that during 1976 the USSR had become one of

Argentina's largest customers despite the absolute fall in volume since 1975. At the initiative of the Soviet delegation, the commission also discussed the necessity of increasing Argentina's purchases from the Soviet Union; Argentina promised to review the recommendation favorably. Finally, the commission stressed the need to ratify agreements already signed and discussed new aspects of cooperation in science, technology, fishing, and air transportation.[49]

The Soviets staged a national exposition in Buenos Aires to coincide with the meeting of the joint commission. Twenty-nine Soviet organizations displayed their wares and succeeded in placing a number of products on the Argentine market.[50] While the exposition was in progress an incident occurred that demonstrated the Argentine government's determination to avoid damaging relations with the Soviet Union. A group of seven Soviet technicians attached to the exposition attended a luncheon hosted by the FATE firm (one of the Gelbard group) in the town of San Fernando. The Russians became involved in a scuffle with some Argentine participants and were jailed. The foreign ministry announced that their visas had been annulled and they would be expelled because they had violated a condition of their entry permits restricting them to Buenos Aires. However, pressure from the economics ministry led to the cancellation of this punitive measure, and the technicians were ultimately allowed to remain in Argentina until the end of the exposition.[51]

At the beginning of 1977 it was announced that the Argentine grain harvest had broken all records; total production of wheat, corn, sorghum, and soybeans was more than 28 million tons (in comparison to 21.5 million tons in 1976),[52] and grain exports had risen from 9 million tons in 1975–76 to 14.5 million tons in 1976–77.[53] Nevertheless, as table 4 shows, Argentine exports to the Soviet Union declined, and the value of Argentine sales to the USSR fell from US$219 million in 1976 to US$211 million in 1977.

The decline in grain sales to the Soviet Union in 1977 was due to Argentina's selling its grain at prices much lower than those prevailing on the North American grain market (averaging US$6.50 less per ton of wheat, for example). As a result, international trading companies such as Dreyfus, Continental Grains, Nirovita, Cargill, and Bunge and Born made large purchases, some of which were probably resold to the Soviet

Union without designating Argentina as the country of origin.[54] Argentine skepticism about the credibility of the trading companies and its need for reliable markets sustaining adequate prices go a long way toward explaining Argentina's later preference for signing intergovernmental agreements on grain purchases. The Soviets also prefer intergovernmental agreements since they eliminate the middleman's take and guarantee continued supply despite price fluctuations.

Soviet imports from Argentina increased in 1977 because of greater purchases of meat. Argentine exports rose from over 11,000 tons in 1976 to 32,138 tons in 1977; the USSR thus absorbed almost 10 percent of Argentina's meat exports and became its third largest customer (after Brazil and West Germany).[55]

In the course of 1977, the Argentine government cemented formal relations by ratifying other agreements which had been pending approval since 1974, including those related to economic-commercial and scientific-commercial cooperation and the delivery of Soviet machinery and equipment.

The joint commission held its third meeting in Moscow in September 1977. The Soviet delegation expressed its satisfaction with the ratification of the agreements but again stressed its concern over the continuing trade deficit and insisted that Argentina increase its purchases. It also insisted that Argentina finally approve contracts for the supply of Soviet machinery and equipment to Yacimientos Carboníferos Fiscales (YCF). Valued at approximately US$30 million, the equipment's delivery had been delayed because Argentine technicians had expressed concern about its quality. The Soviets also insisted on the ratification of the contract signed in 1975—but not ratified by the Peronist government— for the surveying and exploration by Technopromexport of the Middle Paraná hydroelectric project. The Argentines expressed interest in increasing exports of meat, wine, vegetable oils, yarns, hides, and other products. The Soviets expressed willingness to cooperate if and when Argentina increased its purchases from the USSR. Finally, the commission agreed to continue studies on joint research on Argentine fishing resources and the mechanization of hide processing.[56]

A favorable reaction to Soviet demands was not long in coming. On 22 September 1977 General Videla declared that objections to the purchase of Soviet equipment by YCF were unwarranted, and the contract was approved. The contract signed between YCF and Machinoexport had initially provided for the purchase of equipment, tunneling machinery, underground trains, ventilators, and explosives at a value of US$30 million, but it was not ratified by the Peronist government. After the military coup of 1976 the contract was renegotiated, and the purchases were reduced to a value of US$8 million, the amount finally approved.[57]

The most serious incidents in the post-Peronist era occurred between 22 September and 1 October 1977 when the Argentine navy intercepted seven Soviet fishing vessels which, according to Argentine sources, were sailing within the 200-mile territorial limit. Escorted to port and relieved of their cargos, they were obliged to pay heavy fines before being allowed to leave. The Argentine foreign ministry sent a protest to the Soviet embassy stating that the commander of the navy, Admiral Emilio Massera, had ordered the seizures because, in his words, "The defense of our sovereignty is at stake."[58] The Soviet press denied that the fishing vessels had violated the 200-mile limit and attributed the incident to "a premeditated action meant to provoke a clamorous anti-Soviet campaign in the Argentine press," claiming it was part of a plan to block the ratification of pending agreements and contracts.[59] The clamor soon died down, however, and the incident was not brought up again.

Throughout 1978 economic and trading relations between the two countries continued to develop in a climate of mutual agreement (see table 5). During that year the volume of Argentine exports to the USSR began an ascending spiral that reached its peak in the early 1980s. The volume of exports grew by more than 50 percent over 1977, increasing from US$211 million to US$385 million in 1978. This increase was largely due to sharply increased Soviet purchases of wheat (961,000 tons), and to a lesser degree by increased purchases of corn (1.8 million tons). The USSR absorbed 66 percent of all Argentine wheat exports and 30 percent of corn exports.[60] However, Argentine imports from the USSR suffered a decline from their already low figures, falling from US$20.3 million in 1977 to US$11.1 million in 1978, and Argentina again enjoyed a large trade surplus, this time in the amount of US$373.9 million.

As far as contracts were concerned, an agreement was finally signed

Table 5
Soviet Trade with Argentina, 1977–1978
(in thousands of rubles)

	1977	1978
EXPORTS		
Machinery, equipment, and vehicles	10,417	17,638
Electricity-generating equipment	2,660	9,850
Specialized machinery	2,715	—
Storage tanks	3,760	900
Transportation equipment	—	380
Bearings	239	71
Trucks	—	255
Spare parts for trucks	54	73
Sodium dichromate	2,621	2,270
Pharmaceuticals	132	206
Household goods and cultural articles	80	—
Printed matter	62	29
Films	18	9
Total	13,400	22,400
IMPORTS		
Tubes	6,180	3,656
Fine sheep wool	40,174	46,907
Synthetic wool	349	572
Wool textiles	2,681	1,607
Shoe leather	9,437	2,507
Tanned leather	18,990	9,628
Agar-agar	119	111
Wheat	10,800	82,562
Corn	34,397	130,027
Frozen meat	30,703	—
Linseed oil	17,297	12,347
Wine	1,928	3,079
Printed matter	16	15
Total	191,600	308,800

Source: Vneshniaia torgovlia SSSR, statisticheskii sbornik, Annual supplement for 1978.

Note: Totals and the subtotal for machinery exceed sum of partial yearly figures because only the most important items are enumerated in the table.

with Technopromexport to carry out the surveying and design of the Middle Paraná project. The scope of the agreement was reduced, covering only the southern dam at Chapetón at a value of US$4.5 million (US$2 million for equipment and the rest for the study itself). The original agreement, which had been signed but not ratified in 1975, had been for the complete project and had been valued at US$8.2 million.[61] In any case, the contract still put the Soviets in a favorable position when it came time to invite public bids for completing the studies and beginning construction of the dams and hydroelectric stations. This stage began in December 1981 with the call for bids regarding the southern dam project.[62] Relatively conservative sources estimated that total investment in the complex could amount to more than US$9 billion (in 1979 dollars).[63] Soviet participation in a complex with a projected generating capacity of 5 million kilowatts has earned it the nickname "Aswan of Latin America."

Economic relations during 1979 were characterized more by consolidation than by spectacular developments. Argentine exports to the Soviet Union amounted to US$455 million, an increase of only US$70 million over the year before. The most significant difference in comparison with 1978 was a sharp drop in the volume of wheat exported (only 109,000 tons) and a very slight increase in sales of corn (1.8 million tons). However, grain prices rose sharply on the world market, which meant that lesser export volume still earned foreign exchange of value equivalent to that of 1978.[64] On the other hand, exports of frozen beef increased slightly (35,200 tons in 1979 compared to 32,138 tons in 1978), making the Soviet Union the second largest importer of Argentine meat (after Brazil). Since meat prices in 1979 averaged 40 percent more than in 1978, the total value of meat exports was far greater than the slight increase in tonnage would suggest.[65] The Soviets also increased their imports of Argentine tubing, wool, linseed, and linseed oil. (See table 6.)

Soviet exports to Argentina also increased in absolute terms, rising from US$11.1 million in 1978 to US$35.9 million in 1979. This rather large increase was due to new purchases of electricity generating equipment, transportation equipment, trucks, and spare parts and accessories.

Table 6
Argentine Trade with the Soviet Union, 1979–1981
(in thousands of tons and millions of U.S. dollars)

	1979		1980		1981[a]	
	Volume	*Value*	*Volume*	*Value*	*Volume*	*Value*
EXPORTS						
Wheat	109.0	19.58	2,436.0	455.59	2,352.0	617.70
Corn	1,804.0	188.21	3,003.0	428.91	8,013.0	1,281.80
Sorghum	—	—	1,493.0	210.25	3,967.0	587.25
Soybeans	—	—	667.0	163.13	758.0	271.15
Frozen meat	35.2	62.64	84.3	179.66	71.6	159.50
Tung oil	3.0	3.48	5.7	5.22	4.2	5.80
Linseed oil	75.6	40.17	89.0	46.26	93.8	69.60
Sunflower oil	—	—	50.4	30.16	232.2	178.35
Soybean oil	—	—	10.3	5.37	9.9	7.25
Fine wool	16.4	56.41	15.8	63.66	15.3	72.50
Shoe leather[b]	13.1	2.32	14.2	1.89	46.7	5.80
Semiprocessed leather[c]	2.4	24.36	1.8	18.13	1.8	20.30
Quebracho extract	8.1	4.06	10.3	5.37	9.9	7.25
Sugar	—	—	12.5	3.77	106.1	72.50
Tubes	23.9	16.24	4.1	5.08	12.3	21.75
Total	—	418.62	—	1,685.05	—	3,439.40
IMPORTS						
Machinery and equipment	—	31.61	—	37.56	—	37.70
Electricity-generating equipment	—	11.31	—	24.51	—	34.80
Transportation and storage equipment	—	3.92	—	1.74	—	1.02
Sodium dichromate	4.7	3.34	5.3	4.06	5.7	4.93
Total	—	35.96	—	44.08	—	44.95

Sources: Soviet Ministry of Foreign Trade; Secretaría de Comercio de la Argentina; Ministerio de Economía, *Boletín Semanal de Economía,* no. 439 (3 May 1982).

a. Estimated figures.
b. Millions of square decimeters.
c. Millions of square meters.

But the Soviet trade deficit with Argentina also increased to US$418.9 million, or US$45 million more than in 1978.

• The Grain Embargo and the Zenith of Trade

The year 1980 was of decisive importance for the expansion of trade relations between Argentina and the Soviet Union. If the preceding period had been an era of consolidation, 1980 was the year in which trade relations assumed a dizzying rhythm.

Jimmy Carter's attempt to organize an international grain embargo against the USSR in retaliation for the invasion of Afghanistan provided the impetus for the dramatic expansion of Argentine-Soviet trade. On 5 January 1980 the United States announced that it would refuse to sell an additional 17 million tons of grain to the Soviet Union and asked other Western grain-exporting countries to join the embargo. The initial reaction of the Argentine government was to suspend the issuing of new export licenses by the Junta Nacional de Granos (JNG) until the situation had been clarified.[66] It quickly became clear that this decision was meant to prevent a "run" on the Buenos Aires grain exchange.

On 10 January 1980 Argentina announced that it was sending a delegation headed by the director of the JNG, David Lacroze, to Washington to attend the meeting called by Carter to discuss the embargo with the principal grain-exporting countries. But on the same day the Argentine foreign ministry issued a communique stating that the country "refused to take part in punitive decisions adopted without our participation, or which were taken in decision centers outside the country." The communique also stated that it was "a fundamental principle of Argentine foreign policy not to use economic actions as a means of pressure or retaliation."[67]

At the Washington meeting Argentina reiterated its refusal to participate in the embargo. According to the secretary of agriculture, Jorge Horacio Zorreguieta, Argentina expected market forces to determine the final destination of Argentine exports.[68] It was later reported that the government reached its decision not to join the embargo after meeting with members of the country's two most important agricultural organizations, Confederaciones Rurales Argentinas and CONINAGRO, whose representatives stressed the economic advantages of continuing grain sales to the USSR.[69]

Confronted with this situation, Carter sent General Andrew Goodpaster—the former supreme commander of NATO—to Argentina at the end of January in an effort to convince the Argentine military to reverse its decision. His mission was unsuccessful, and Argentina continued its grain exports to the Soviet Union.[70]

At this time a double movement of prices and potential buyers began to develop on the international grain market. Quotations for Argentine grains began to rise rapidly, while U.S. grain prices fell sharply (a ton of corn, for example, averaged US$140 in Buenos Aires and US$107.50 in Chicago). As a result, Western buyers gravitated to the United States because of the lower prices, while the USSR, having no choice, looked to Argentina for its grain purchases.[71]

Shortly after Goodpaster's departure, a delegation from the Soviet commercial firm Export-Khleb arrrived in Argentina to supervise the shipment of grain already purchased and to initiate negotiations for the purchase of the largest possible additional quantity. As the only customer willing to buy high-priced Argentine grain in large quantities, the Soviet delegation had no problem in fulfilling its mission.[72] On this first occasion the Soviets agreed to buy 2.9 million tons of corn, amounting to more than 80 percent of Argentina's exportable surplus.[73]

Between February and March 1980 negotiations were held on the purchase of other grains, including wheat and sorghum.[74] The Soviets ultimately bought 2.3 million tons of wheat (or 50 percent of the total exported by Argentina in 1980), and 1.5 million tons of sorghum (98 percent of total exports), as well as large quantities of soybeans (747,000 tons). The Soviet Union thus emerged as the largest purchaser of Argentine grains, absorbing 60 percent of Argentina's total grain exports in 1980 (7.6 million tons of various grains out of a total of 12.6 million tons).[75]

The conditions under which these purchases were made—with the Soviet Union paying an "embargo premium"—provided Argentina with an estimated US$1 billion in foreign exchange over what it would have obtained under normal market conditions.[76] By the end of 1980 the value of Argentine exports to the Soviet Union had risen to US$1.685

billion. In contrast, Soviet exports to Argentina totaled only US$44 million, providing Argentina with a trade surplus of US$1.641 billion.[77]

In April 1980 the Argentine-Soviet joint commission met in Buenos Aires and announced that the USSR would continue its imports of Argentina grains and would also give priority to meat purchases.[78] The two countries also announced that they had agreed to establish more permanent mechanisms to assure the continuation of trade; the Soviet Union once again stressed its desire to reduce the disequilibrium in the balance of trade.

Soviet plans to increase meat purchases were soon realized, and by the end of 1980 the Soviet Union had bought 131,000 tons, nearly triple the amount purchased in 1979 and a major factor in the gigantic increase in the value of Argentine exports to the USSR.[79]

In July 1980 the previous agreement to establish a more permanent framework for continued trade found concrete expression in a medium-term agreement governing the sale of Argentine grain to the Soviet Union. This agreement provided for the sale of 22.5 million tons of Argentine grain in the following five years, or 4.5 million tons annually.[80] Of these 4.5 million tons, 3 million were to be corn, 1 million sorghum, and the 500,000 remaining tons soybeans. The grain was to be purchased by Export-Khleb from Argentine firms at prices prevailing on the international market at the time of shipment. It was further agreed that these figures represented minimum export quantities and could be increased by agreement if required. Interestingly, wheat was not included in the agreement despite large Soviet purchases of that grain in 1980, probably because of the greater ease with which Argentina could find buyers for wheat on the international market.

Soviet exports to Argentina consisted mainly of heavy machinery and transportation equipment—including the first shipment of trackless trolleys for the city of Rosario, electricity generating equipment, spare parts and accessories, and other types of manufactured products.[81]

• The Consolidation of Bilateral Relations

During 1981 relations between the two countries continued to be extremely productive, especially with regard to new agreements and the increase of Argentine exports, although there was also a greater diversification of Soviet sales.

In January 1981 Argentina announced that it had purchased five tons of heavy water from the USSR for use in the Atucha I nuclear power plant, and that negotiations were under way on the possibility of enriching uranium for use in experimental nuclear reactors.[82] The purchase of heavy water was undertaken to guarantee an adequate supply pending the completion of a production facility being built in Arroyito (Neuquén Province) under the direction of the Swiss firm Sulzner Brothers. It was also announced that the material had been bought under the system of safeguards established by the International Atomic Energy Commission.

The lifting of the grain embargo against the USSR, announced by President Reagan in April 1981, had no significant impact on the volume of Argentine-Soviet trade. The Soviets, viewing Argentina as a reliable supplier of grain, preferred to complete their negotiations with Argentina before opening talks with the United States, whom they accused of having lost credibility as a supplier, even though Argentine production could not totally cover Soviet needs resulting from the poor harvests between 1978 and 1981.[83]

In April 1981 an Argentine-Soviet agreement was signed providing for the export of an average of 60,000 to 100,000 tons of boneless beef annually for a period of five years.[84] The protocol signed by the Argentine ambassador in Moscow, Leopoldo Bravo, and the Soviet minister of commerce, Nikolai Patolichev, provided for an initial price of US$2,000 per ton, which could be adjusted by agreement in response to market conditions. The quantities mentioned in the agreement were a guideline and could be increased as required, and the agreement could be extended. The Argentine minister of trade, Carlo García Martínez, called the agreement "the largest contract of the past few years" and noted that, in addition to opening new markets, it also provided for some stability in what had otherwise been an erratic international market. By the end of 1981 the Soviets had exceeded the fixed quota and become Argentina's largest customer, with purchases amounting to 113,800 tons of meat. Sales to the Soviets represented 21.5 percent of total meat exports and 35 percent of chilled meat exports.[85]

In May 1981 a Soviet mission headed by the vice-minister for foreign trade, Boris Gordeiev, and the president of Export-Khleb, Viktor Pershin, arrived in Argentina to hold talks on the grain and meat trade, study the possibility of purchases of wines, fruits, and tobacco, and attempt to increase Argentine purchases of Soviet equipment and machinery.[86] The Soviet delegation visited the cities of Mendoza, Rosario, San Juan, and Buenos Aires, holding talks with provincial and national authorities. As a result of these meetings, the Soviets agreed to increase purchases of grain; contracts were signed for the export of 7 million tons of corn and sorghum, 2.5 million tons of wheat, 700,000 tons of soybeans, and 100,000 tons of oats. This amounted to a total of more than 10 million tons, which far exceeded the quantity established in the five-year agreement signed the year before. The Soviets also mentioned the possibility of buying an additional 3 million tons of corn and sorghum, which would triple the volume of exports to the USSR in 1980. Referring to the lifting of the U.S. grain embargo, the Soviets emphasized that "Argentina would continue to be Moscow's prime supplier" because "the lifting of the embargo does not restore the *status quo ante*" and that the USSR granted Argentina "absolute priority when it comes to grain purchases."[87]

In June 1981 an Argentine delegation headed by the minister of trade, García Martínez, and the secretaries of foreign trade, A. Espósito, and agriculture, V. Santirso, visited the USSR to attend the fifth meeting of the Argentine-Soviet joint commission.[88] The delegation was received by the president of the Soviet Council of Ministers, Nikolai Tijonov, who pointed out that the meeting was a "memorable event," coming as it did on the thirty-fifth anniversary of the establishment of diplomatic relations. He also referred to Argentina as "a very reliable trading partner" and remarked that this reliability would be kept very much in mind with regard to "forthcoming purchases by the Soviet Union."

The protocol signed at the end of the meeting provided that the USSR would purchase all the krill caught in the South Atlantic that Argentina did not consume itself; the second point stipulated that technicians would be exchanged to carry out the maritime and merchant shipping programs; in the third point the Soviet Union promised to study the possibility of increasing the minimum quantities of grain and meat to be purchased from Argentina. It was also announced that in September 1981 a group of Argentine officials would visit the Soviet Union to study the expansion of purchases of Soviet products and the possibility of granting the Soviets greater participation in the study of the Middle Paraná project. Finally, Argentina agreed to purchase machinery, equipment, and other Soviet products at a value of US$500 million in the 1982–85 period, and to try to purchase US$50 million worth of Soviet goods in 1981.[89]

Figures on total grain exports to the USSR were released in 1982, revealing that exports of corn had reached a volume of 8 million tons (90 percent of total exports); wheat, 2.3 million tons (65 percent of total exports); sorghum, 4 million tons (60 percent of total exports); soybeans, 758,000 tons (30 percent of total exports); oats, 79,000 tons (60 percent of total exports); rye, 49,000 tons (100 percent of total exports). The Soviets were once again the largest single importer of Argentine grains, accounting for 80 percent of Argentina's total exports, or 16 million tons out of a total of 20.5 million.[90] (See table 7.)

In September 1981 it was announced that one of the contracts for the joint Argentine-Paraguayan hydroelectric project at Yaciretá had been awarded to the Yaciretá-Apipé consortium, whose members included Siemens (West Germany), GIE (Italy), and Energomashexport (USSR).[91] The contract called for the consortium to deliver ten generators at a total value of US$51 million, to be financed at an annual interest of 4 percent. Payment was to be made over a period of approximately ten years, to begin once the equipment was installed. A US$46.2 million contract for another ten generators was awarded to the Japan-Voith consortium, formed by Mitsubishi, Hitachi, Toshiba, and Fuji (Japan) and J. M. Voth (West Germany). A third contract for twenty turbines was awarded to the consortium formed by Allis Chalmers (United States) and Metanac (Argentina). One of the firms whose bid was rejected (Canadian General Electric) denounced the decision as completely illogical, claiming that the Japanese, German, and Soviet generators were of poor quality and that its bid had been lower than the others. Argentina and Paraguay ignored the protest, and a short time later the result of the invitation for bids was declared valid in Buenos Aires.[92]

The Soviets also delivered the parts for the second turbogenerator for the Ingeniero White thermoelectric power plant at Bahía Blanca, meaning installation would be complete in 1982 (see table 8).[93]

In March 1982 it was announced that Argentina was sending uranium to the USSR for enrichment.[94] Vice Admiral Castro Madero, president of the National Commission on Atomic Energy, explained that the decision had been taken because of the difficulties encountered in having the material processed in the United States. The shipment consisted of 100 kilograms of natural uranium to be used in a reactor for the production of isotopes; the enrichment was supposedly to be on the order of 20 percent and therefore unsuitable for the development of nuclear weapons.

In April 1982, at the sixth meeting of the joint commission in Buenos Aires, it was announced that the volume of Argentine-Soviet trade had exceeded US\$3 billion in 1981 (see table 6).[95] During the meeting

Table 7

Argentine Exports of Meat and Grain to the Soviet Union, 1970–1981
(in thousands of tons)

	Wheat	*Corn*	*Sorghum*	*Soybeans*	*Beef*
1970	—	—	18.9	—	—
1971	—	280.2	—	—	—
1972	—	—	—	—	—
1973	215.5	190.7	45.7	—	—
1974	747.4	843.3	—	—	16.4
1975	940.1	434.7	—	—	30.8
1976	99.9	251.2	29.7	—	17.0
1977	1,122.7	432.1	—	—	48.0
1978	960.7	1,771.1	—	33.2	—
1979	109.0	1,804.0	—	—	49.0
1980	2,436.0	3,003.0	1,493.0	667.0	131.0
1981a	2,352.0	8,013.0	3,967.0	758.0	71.6

Sources: Junta Nacional de Carnes; Junta Nacional de Granos; Secretaría de Comercio Exterior (Argentina); Ministry of Foreign Trade (USSR).

a. Estimated figures.

Table 8
Argentine Projects with Soviet Participation, as of 1982

1974

Salto Grande hydroelectric station (14 Kaplan-type turbines with a total generating capacity of 1600MW). Completion expected in 1982. Total estimated cost: US$179 million.

1974–1978

Three thermoelectric stations, one to be located in Puerto Nuevo (Buenos Aires) and two in Bahía Blanca (Buenos Aires Province), each with a total capacity of 310MW. The Puerto Nuevo plant is already in operation, one of the Bahía Blanca plants is being installed (Ingeniero White), and construction on the third began in 1982. Total estimated cost: US$77 million.

1975

Cold-lamination train for the manufacture of tubes. Total estimated cost: US$3 million.

1975–1977

Coal-mining equipment for Yacimiento Carboníferos Fiscales in Río Turbio. Total estimated cost of first contract (not ratified): US$30 million; of renegotiated contract: US$8 million.

1975–1978

Design and surveying of the Middle Paraná dam built by Technopromexport. Total estimated cost of first contract (not ratified): US$8.2 million; of second, partial contract, only for the southern dam (Chapeton): US$4.5 million.

1981

Ten generators for the Yaciretá hydroelectric dam, a joint Argentine-Paraguayan project to be constructed by the Yaciretá-Agipé consortium formed by Energomachexport (USSR), Siemens AG (West Germany), and GIE (Italy). (Another ten generators are being constructed by Mitsubishi-Hitachi-Toshiba-Fuji (Japan) and J. M. Voith (West Germany). The turbines are being supplied by a consortium formed by Allis Chalmers (United States) and METANAC and AFNE (Argentina). Total estimated cost: US$51.4 million.

Anticipated contracts

Erection of 500MW electrical transmission lines between San Nicholás and Buenos Aires; hydroelectric plants for the Middle Paraná complex (2,300MW and 3,000MW), at an estimated cost of US$4.5 billion; a complete refinery for petroleum products; a catalytic cracking plant for the production of special gasoline; a cotton fiber factory with 3,000 spindles; expansion of the Chocón-Cerros Colorados hydroelectric dam and the Alicura complex in Río Negro; construction of a fishing port (Punta Quilla) and the creation of joint fishing enterprises.

Soviet delegates yet again expressed their concern with the low level of Argentine purchases and requested that the promises to increase imports made at the last meeting be honored; at the same time they expressed satisfaction that Yacimientos Petrolíferos Fiscales (YPF) had recently decided to purchase US$20 million, and Gas del Estado, US$3 million worth of Soviet equipment and machinery. The Soviet delegation was also optimistic that Agua y Energía Eléctrica and Ferrocarriles Argentinos would purchase goods in the amount of US$30 million. The commission also agreed to extend the agreement on delivery of machinery and equipment until 1985, changing the rates of interest to 6 percent and 6.5 percent annually for state-owned and private enterprises, respectively. Argentina emphasized its interest in raising the minimum volume of grain purchases agreed to by the USSR and in increasing exports of meat, wines, fruits, and juices. The Soviets expressed their desire to send permanent representatives of Prodintorg, Export-Khleb, and the ministry of fisheries to Buenos Aires and organize an office of economic consultation in its embassy; of participating in the construction of the Middle Paraná project, for which they had already submitted a bid in 1982; of signing an agreement of cooperation between Aeroflot and Aerolíneas Argentinas; and of sending a scientific vessel to explore fishing possibilities in the western South Atlantic, with the participation of Argentina and with a view to developing joint fishing ventures. Finally, it was agreed that the next meeting would be held in Moscow in April 1983.

• The Balance of Economic Relations

Analysis of economic and trade relations between Argentina and the Soviet Union from the beginning of the 1970s reveals that the structure had changed substantially in comparison with the pre-1970 period.

The fact that the USSR had come to be the principal individual customer for Argentine exports, while the volume of Soviet sales to Argentina remained very low, indicates that Argentina is practicing a nonreciprocal trading pattern in which the foreign exchange earned by sales to the USSR is used to purchase goods from other countries, such as the members of the Common Market, the United States and Canada, the Latin American nations, and Japan. For example, during 1980 Argentine imports totaled US$10.541 billion: the EEC countries accounted for US$2.846 billion; the United States and Canada for US$2.476 billion; the Latin American countries for US$2.265 billion; Japan for US$1.031 billion and the OPEC countries for US$251.4 million. In contrast, Soviet imports amounted to US$14.7 million. However, the Soviet Union absorbed 33.7 percent of Argentine exports (US$1.614 billion), while the nine members of the EEC accounted for 27.1 percent (US$2.172 billion); the members of the Latin American Free Trade Association (LAFTA), 24.8 percent (US$1.986 billion); the United States and Canada, 9.2 percent (US$738.5 million); and Japan, 2.6 percent (US$210.9 million). (See tables 9, 10, and 11.)

These figures reveal at least three processes that have altered the structure of Argentine foreign trade over the last thirty years: First, the principal customer for Argentine exports is no longer an important supplier of Argentina's imports, as had been the case with England or the European nations, which continued to make large sales in the Argentine market even after their displacement by the United States as Argentina's chief supplier.[96]

Second, manufactured and semimanufactured goods have been declining—or at best only slowly increasing—as a proportion of total Argentine exports, in contrast to previous periods when government economic policy promoted industrialization and the export of manufactured products.[97] Since 1976, manufactured products have taken a back seat in the government's export drive, largely because its orthodox liberal economic strategy is based on the theory of comparative advantage and the supposed benefits of the free market. Argentina's frontiers have been thrown open to foreign competition, protectionist measures have been abolished, and the peso has been allowed to float to its "real" market value. As a result, Argentina has returned to being a specialist in agricultural production because manufacturers have been unable to compete against the low prices and diversified products offered by the developed industrial countries.[98]

Finally, the previous policy of diversifying export markets was reversed in favor of concentrating sales in one purchaser. In part, the huge sales to the USSR in 1980 and 1981 were the unintended result of a

Table 9
Evolution of Argentine Foreign Trade: Exports, 1938–1981
(in billions of current U.S. dollars, annual average over a five-year period)

	Total World Exports	Argentine Exports	% of Total	Argentine Exports to:					
				Brazil	South Africa	Korea	Canada	Australia
1938	23.5	0.4	1.86	—	—	—	0.8	0.6
1948	57.5	1.7	2.89	—	—	—	3.1	1.3
1953	75.5	1.1	1.45	1.5	1.4	0.0	4.4	2.0
1956–60	102.0	1.0	0.98	1.3	1.8	0.0	5.4	2.0
1961–65	140.7	1.3	0.92	1.4	2.4	0.1	7.1	2.7
1966–70	224.3	1.6	0.71	2.1	3.2	0.5	13.0	3.8
1971–75	557.5	2.8	0.50	6.0	5.7	3.1	26.9	8.9
1976–80	1,297.0	6.3	0.49	14.0	15.0	12.6	51.7	16.3
1981[a]	1,809.5	9.2	0.51	23.2	21.0	21.1	72.4	22.0

Source: Secretaría de Comercio de la República Argentina. Ministerio de Economía, Boletín Semanal de Economía, no. 446 (21 June 1982).

a. Estimated figures.

Table 10
Destination of Argentine Exports, 1965–1981
(in billions of current U.S. dollars, annual average over a five-year period)

	1965–69		1970–75		1975–79		1980		1981[a]	
	$	%	$	%	$	%	$	%	$	%
Soviet Union	52.2	3.5	76.2	3.0	303.8	5.7	1,614.2	20.1	2,909.5	33.7
EEC (Common Market)	731.7	58.6	1,038.4	41.0	1,713.4	32.0	2,172.4	27.1	1,817.6	21.1
Latin America	308.0	20.4	627.7	24.8	1,523.9	28.5	1,986.0	24.8	1,708.8	19.8
USA & Canada	131.5	8.7	224.7	8.9	408.3	7.8	738.5	9.2	852.8	9.9
Rest of Europe	122.7	8.1	177.1	7.0	469.6	8.8	372.1	4.6	345.3	4.0
OPEC[b]	31.2	2.1	38.7	1.5	58.6	1.1	175.6	2.2	240.2	2.8
Eastern Europe	46.6	3.1	56.1	2.2	99.8	1.9	197.2	2.5	146.7	1.7
Japan	41.0	2.7	113.9	4.5	285.8	5.3	210.9	2.6	151.6	1.8
Africa	1.9	0.1	39.6	1.6	157.3	2.9	163.1	2.0	167.9	1.9
Asia	38.2	2.5	124.2	4.9	313.2	5.9	384.2	4.8	273.6	3.2
Oceania	1.2	0.1	14.4	0.6	4.0	0.1	7.2	0.1	10.1	0.1
Total	1,506.2	100	2,530.3	100	5,347.7	100	8,021.4	100	8,623.2	100

Source: Secretaría de Comercio de la República Argentina. Ministerio de Economía, Boletín Semanal de Economía, no. 446 (21 June 1982).

a. January–November.
b. Excluding Ecuador and Venezuela.

Table 11
Origin of Argentine Imports, 1965–1981
(in billions of current U.S. dollars, annual average over a five-year period)

	1965–69		1970–74		1975–70		1980		1981[a]	
	$	%	$	%	$	%	$	%	$	%
Soviet Union	12.3	1.0	5.5	0.2	19.4	0.4	14.7	0.1	8.8	0.3
EEC (Common Market)	313.8	25.5	681.0	30.1	1,215.2	28.0	2,846.4	27.2	683.4	26.3
Latin America	296.8	24.1	489.4	21.6	1,081.9	24.9	2,265.0	21.5	683.4	26.3
USA & Canada	313.9	25.5	516.6	22.8	904.3	20.8	2,476.9	23.6	627.8	24.0
Rest of Europe	116.1	9.4	166.3	7.3	350.8	8.1	915.8	8.1	198.8	7.6
OPEC[b]	60.3	4.5	95.3	4.2	165.5	3.8	251.4	2.4	97.2	3.7
Eastern Europe	13.0	1.1	36.3	1.6	56.8	1.3	80.1	0.8	25.3	1.0
Japan	44.5	3.6	206.7	9.1	346.2	8.0	1,031.2	9.8	328.9	12.6
Africa	25.5	2.1	14.6	0.6	59.2	1.4	110.1	1.0	17.5	0.7
Oceania	2.2	0.2	8.4	0.4	53.8	1.2	93.4	0.9	18.7	0.7
Total	1,252.7	100	2,266.2	100	4,337.2	100	10,541.0	100	2,614.0	100

Source: Secretaría de Comercio de la República Argentina. Ministerio de Economía, *Boletín Semanal de Economía*, no. 439 (3 May 1982).

Note: Percentages may not add up to 100 because of rounding.

a. January–March.
b. Excluding Ecuador and Venezuela.

policy begun in 1971 to reduce Argentine dependency on a few unstable markets by opening new ones in the socialist bloc. The end result, however, has been to substitute one country for what had been a group of purchasers; the potential dangers of this situation are partially redressed by the long-term stability and volume of the transactions.

All the above suggests a certain Argentine vulnerability in its trade relations with the USSR, a vulnerability of which both parties are fully aware. The first danger is that, after absorbing huge quantities of Argentine exports for a certain period of time, the USSR will reduce its purchases because of the availability of lower prices elsewhere or an increase in its own agricultural production. The Soviets have assured the Argentines that they are its preferred suppliers of meat and grain, but trade agreements have set minimum quotas that have been far exceeded in recent years. If the Soviets were to limit purchases to the fixed quotas, Argentine producers would find themselves in a difficult situation. Accordingly, Argentina has tried to increase the minimum quotas fixed by agreement; the Soviets have declined, at least for the time being. On the other hand, an increase in Soviet food production seems highly unlikely; even the most optimistic projections point to stabilization of production as the best that can be hoped for, meaning imports would have to continue at current levels.[99]

Relying on an individual customer of this magnitude continues to worry the Argentines; as the subsecretary of international economic negotiations during 1981 emphasized, "Depending on a single large purchaser is not a comfortable policy."[100] The Argentine press has devoted considerable attention to this issue. *Clarín* has commented that trade relations with the Soviet Union are now similar to the dependent relations Argentina had with Britain until the end of World War II, with the exception that—in contrast to Britain—Argentine imports represent only a small proportion of total Soviet consumption.[101] An article in the Argentine magazine *Ultima Clave* in 1980 described sales to the USSR as having evolved from an attractive deal to an unavoidable necessity, with all the consequences that implies.[102] In 1981 *La Nación* expressed fear that excessive dependence on one customer could open the way to political pressure or put the country in a difficult position if trade had to be suspended for whatever reason.[103] Finally, a 1981 editorial in the *Buenos Aires Herald* called increased economic and trade ties with the Soviet Union a trap that would oblige Argentina to align itself with the Soviets in the international political arena.[104]

Another factor worrying the Argentines is that negotiations for purchase—but not the agreements—are conducted between the Soviet state monopoly, Export-Khleb, and various Argentine sellers, which gives the former the upper hand in bargaining. In a comment referring to meat sales, but which can also be applied to grain, the president of the Cámara Argentina de Frigoríficos Industriales y Exportadores de Carne, Luis Bameule, said that it was necessary to "consolidate Argentine supply in response to consolidated Soviet demand . . . because the opposite would produce an undesirable imbalance in negotiations."[105] This proposal was rejected by the economics ministry, which was hostile to the creation of a state marketing institution similar to IAPI; the ministry expected that an imbalance in negotiating power could be avoided because prices were fixed by the international market and not by political or economic pressure.

Another problem caused by the increase in exports to the Soviet Union is Argentina's withdrawal from other traditional markets, to which it would be difficult to return if sales to the USSR were to decrease significantly.

The danger of being exposed to economic and political pressures from the USSR was alluded to by the Argentine minister of foreign trade, García Martínez, when he noted that the goal of diversifying trade should not be abandoned, in order to prevent "any one market in particular from assuming such importance that it could impose political or ideological dependency on the country."[106] While the Soviets have not put political pressure on Argentina, they have exerted economic pressure, suggesting with greater vehemence in 1980–81 that increased Soviet imports would be strongly linked to Argentina's willingness to increase its purchases of Soviet products.

Aside from official foot-dragging, another problem that has hampered the placement of Soviet products in Argentina is connected with installation services, advice and supervision by technicians in installing equipment, the availability of spare parts and accessories, and skepticism concerning the quality of Soviet machinery. However, problems with installation, technical assistance, and obtaining spare parts have turned out to be less serious than originally anticipated, and relations between technicians from the two countries have developed amicably, permitting projects to be completed on time.

Problems have developed, however, over the substandard quality or poor performance of some equipment, especially hydroelectric equipment. In June 1980 the second Soviet turbine installed at Salto Grande caught fire after only 4,000 hours of operation, and the third turbine proved to be inadequately lubricated during its trial run and had to be repaired.[107] In August 1981 the Argentine state enterprise AFNE reported that it had had to repair the drive shaft of the generator of the tenth turbine at Salto Grande because it was showing signs of wear.[108] Situations of this type led to criticism of the quality of Soviet equipment in some publications, including *La Prensa* and *Convicción* (Argentina), *El Día* (Uruguay), and *Newsweek* (United States).[109] This barrage of criticism ultimately forced General Viviani Rossi, the Argentine representative on the joint Argentine-Uruguayan commission for Salto Grande, to declare in defense of Argentina's trade partner that the quality of the Soviet turbines was among the best in the world.[110]

The advantages Argentina enjoys in its economic relations with the Soviet Union have been enumerated throughout this chapter and can be briefly recapitulated: medium-term guarantees on sales of meat and grain; payment for purchases in hard currency and at prices prevailing on the world market; the ability to purchase machinery and equipment at advantageous prices and financing terms; an alternative source of nuclear materials, including heavy water and enriched uranium; and the acquisition of technology and scientific know-how necessary to expand certain little-developed economic activities, such as mining and fishing.

From the Soviet point of view, economic relations with Argentina offer a number of advantages and disadvantages. The signing of contracts for the provision of meat and grain allows the Soviets to circumvent other Western suppliers who subject their sales to political preconditions. Sales of equipment and machinery to Argentina represent the opening of a new, stable market that had long been closed to Soviet goods, or at best imported them erratically. Although Argentine purchases are currently meager in comparison to the volume of Soviet imports, the possibility of participating in huge projects such as the

Middle Paraná complex is highly attractive. Another important factor is the Soviet expectation that trade with Argentina will have a demonstration effect on other Latin American countries, convincing them of the benefits of bilateral contacts and thus opening additional new markets.

On the negative side, the main Soviet difficulty is its enormous trade deficit, which has been increasing rapidly. Since this represents a drain on Soviet hard currency reserves, it is readily understandable why Soviet negotiators insist on some degree of reciprocity in purchases, even though they realize that their ultimate goal of a trade balance will take a long time to achieve. On the other hand, the Argentine preference for making purchases by means of international calls-for-bids runs up against the Soviet preference for bilateral contracts that avoid the insecurities and international inspections of the multilateral system. Moreover, although Argentina has shown itself to be a reliable supplier, making full deliveries on schedule, it has been unreliable in its agreements to import Soviet goods, often putting off purchases because of balance-of-payments problems or supposed technical difficulties.

Another factor that could complicate Soviet relations with Argentina is the latter's interest in acquiring nuclear material from the USSR. The Soviets tend to be extremely cautious in supplying such material and very strict in enforcing international safeguards. Thus, although the Argentines have insisted they would use nuclear materials only for peaceful purposes, the Soviets have shown little enthusiasm for expanding sales of this type or increasing their technical assistance to Argentina's nuclear development program.

Finally, a further problem for the Soviets is Argentina's potential unreliability as a supplier. Although Argentine good will is taken for granted, international crises such as the Malvinas conflict, political or social disturbances, or poor harvests could force Argentina to reduce its exports. Since the Argentine share of total Soviet grain imports increased from 14 percent in 1979 to 30 percent in 1981, the Soviets are understandably concerned about any developments that might cut off the Argentine supply.[111] If Argentine shipments failed to reach Soviet ports, the USSR would be forced to look quickly for other suppliers in the international market, producing price increases and reproducing on a lesser scale a situation similar to that of the 1980 grain embargo.

3 Converging Interests: Diplomacy and Military Contacts

• Diplomatic Relations: Between Friction and Rapprochement

The expansion of economic relations between Argentina and the Soviet Union during the 1970s was accompanied by progress in the diplomatic and military spheres and had a significant impact on Argentine political life. As economic ties grew and deepened, a web of other converging interests was spun, sometimes openly, sometimes discreetly.

As we discussed in the previous chapter, Lanusse's arrival in the presidency in 1971 marked the beginning of a new era in Argentine foreign policy. His diplomatic strategy involved abandoning the doctrine of "ideological frontiers" and its substitution by the concept of "ideological pluralism." Consequently, closer ties were forged with the reformist South American regimes of the era and with the nations of the Andean Pact. Argentina also set out to develop closer relations with the other countries of the River Plate region (Uruguay and Paraguay) in an attempt to progressively isolate the Brazilian military regime within Latin America because of its aggressive, possibly threatening foreign policy.[1] To achieve these objectives, Lanusse met with Salvador Allende and extended credits to Chile, and visited a number of Latin American countries (Colombia, Ecuador, Mexico, Peru, and Venezuela) to reestablish friendly contacts.

Outside the hemisphere, the new foreign policy led to the diplomatic recognition of the People's Republic of China in February 1972 and the establishment of more cordial relations with the countries of the Third World and the socialist bloc.

The Lanusse government reopened negotiations on the trade agreement that had been worked out during Illia's presidency and allowed to lapse under Onganía. Nevertheless, signing of the agreement had no important economic or diplomatic consequences.[2] Its major tangible effect was to ease tensions between the two countries, whose relations had recently been upset by incidents such as the expulsion of diplomats, exchange of protests, and repeated attacks on the Soviet embassy and its personnel. Alleged violations of Argentine territorial waters by Soviet fishing vessels continued, but these incidents were settled with greater discretion and were not accompanied by anti-Soviet campaigns in the press.

The most important aspect of this new stage in relations was not economic or trade agreements, but the fact that an Argentine military government had initiated the opening to the East. Since the October Revolution of 1917, the Argentine military had assumed an intransigent anticommunist position that made no distinction between local communists, the international communist movement, and the USSR, the latter of which was blamed for all social protest movements within the country. Accordingly, whenever they were in power, the military severed or froze all contacts with the Soviet Union; out of power, they pressured civilian governments to do the same.[3]

The Lanusse government's pragmatism not only implied the abandonment of a long tradition, but also made it easier for subsequent governments to expand relations with the Soviet Union. The military and those civilian sectors that constitute the "permanent club of coup instigators"—in the sense that they promote coups and repeatedly occupy key positions in the cabinets of military government[4]—might be thought to be uncomfortable with this new situation, since it neutralized one of their most effective weapons for destabilizing civilian governments. Although such fears—supposed or real—have been expressed periodically, it seems that the putschist sectors have abandoned the anti-Soviet argument, at least as a weapon in their destabilizing arsenal. For this reason alone the Lanusse government's foreign policy shift represented a profound change that would affect later developments.

• The Return of Peronism and the "Third Position"

With the Peronist return to power in May 1973, the opening to the socialist countries was consolidated, for both pragmatic and political reasons.

The doctrine of the "Third Position" was a logical extension of "ideological pluralism" and was implemented vigorously by the new government. The "Programmatic Guidelines for the Justicialist Government of National Reconstruction," published in January 1973, defined the "Third Position" as "a concept distinct from both individualism and collectivism, both equally materialist and inhuman, [while] Peronist Doctrine [is] profoundly Christian and humanist." Furthermore, the "Third Position would allow the country to adopt "an attitude uncompromised by and equidistant from the two imperialisms" [the USSR and the United States].[5]

The same document announced that relations would be opened with all countries, including, obviously, the socialist nations. The presidents of Cuba, Osvaldo Dorticós, and of Chile, Salvador Allende, were specially invited guests at Cámpora's inauguration on 25 May 1973,[6] and in his inaugural message to Congress Cámpora repeated his intention to follow the "Programmatic Guidelines" in his foreign policy.[7] On 28 May 1973 diplomatic relations were reestablished with Cuba, and in June relations were established with North Korea and the German Democratic Republic.[8] The "Gelbard Mission" later visited Cuba, which was granted a US$1.2 billion loan.[9]

Cámpora's replacement by Lastiri was related to domestic problems and had no appreciable effect on foreign policy, even though the Peronist left had been replaced in the cabinet by right-wingers. The Lastiri government's most important foreign policy initiative was to apply for membership in the nonaligned movement, which Argentina joined in August 1973. The communique issued by the Argentine foreign ministry on this occasion emphasized that this step was consistent with the "Third Position" and assured that Argentina would participate actively in the work of the organization and contribue to the struggle against new forms of colonialism and exploitation.[10]

A series of events in Latin America in 1973, including the overthrow of Allende in Chile and the military coup in Uruguay, help to explain the rapprochement between Argentina and the Soviet Union. Peronist analysis of the situation saw Argentina being surrounded by a "ring" of authoritarian regimes headed by Brazil (and probably at the service of the United States), which behooved Argentina to find allies among the nonaligned and socialist countries, especially the USSR.[11] The Soviets, for their part, regarded the new South American situation as negatively affecting their interests and harshly criticized the military governments of Chile and Uruguay.[12] Argentina, on the other hand, was looked on favorably for its neutralist foreign policy and moderately progressive domestic policy. In the Soviet view, expanded relations with Argentina could partially make up for the setback suffered in the coup against Allende.[13]

The Soviet press now abandoned all references to Perón as a pro-fascist and began to describe his regime as progressive. An article published in Moscow after Perón's death in July 1974 said that he "had changed much in eighteen years of exile," and that "when the military dictatorship fell [referring to that of 1966–73] and the Peronists returned to power, the constitutional government proclaimed a policy of democratizing the institutions of the country, attacking the activities of the foreign monopolies and restricting the privileges of the land-owning oligarchy. . . . A number of companies were nationalized [and] Argentina began to implement an independent foreign policy and to expand its relations with the socialists countries," which "augmented Peron's prestige and earned him the support of the major parties of the 'constructive opposition,' including the communists."[14]

The visit to Argentina of the Soviet trade mission in February 1974 and the visit of the Gelbard mission to Moscow in May 1974 permitted discussions that went beyond the expansion of trade.[15] The Argentine delegation, which included among its members officials from the ministries of economics and foreign relations, members of Congress, representatives of the armed forces, and business executives engaged in a number of diplomatic exchanges. Gelbard also used the visit to discuss political issues, decorated Brezhnev, Podgorny, and Kosygin with the Great Cross of the Order of the May Revolution—the highest Argentine honor—and made arrangements for a visit by Perón in September 1974 (which never occurred because of his death on 1 July 1974). Both parties agreed that the meeting had laid the groundwork for long-term cooperation and emphasized repeatedly that bilateral relations had entered a new stage.[16]

The Argentine-Soviet meetings were beneficial to both parties from a diplomatic point of view. For the USSR they represented new access to the southern cone, through one of the most important countries in the area. In addition to the contacts made during the visits, the meetings opened the possibility of establishing closer ties, over a period of time, with persons and institutions outside the strictly economic sphere. On a more indirect level, good relations with Argentina guaranteed that the latter would maintain its trade with Cuba, thus partially relieving the USSR of the burden of propping up the Cuban economy, whose difficulties had worsened because of the trade embargo imposed on it by the majority of American nations. Finally, relations with Argentina implied a simultaneous weakening of its ties with the United States, as Soviet publications observed with satisfaction in their praise of the Peronist government's anti-imperialist posture.[17]

From the Argentine perspective, relations with the Soviet Union offered a diplomatic advantage by sharpening its profile as a country with a distinct, independent foreign policy—and thereby one worthy of a leadership role in Latin America in contrast to Brazil, with its decidedly pro-U.S. foreign policy. Argentina hoped further that its neutralist position would permit it to obtain political and economic benefits by playing the Western, socialist, and Third World countries off against each other, in some cases using the threat of tilting toward one of the other blocs, in other cases taking advantage of its apparent neutrality regarding disputes between the superpowers. Moreover, the diplomatic opening to the USSR had domestic political value in that it could be used to placate the most radical Peronist factions and the left (including, of course, the PCA), who were unhappy with certain aspects of the government's domestic social and economic policy.

The death of Perón in July 1974 quickly cleared the way for a political, economic, and social crisis that adversely affected relations with the USSR. The minister of social welfare, López Rega, typically exceeded his ostensible portfolio to implement changes in foreign policy. His primary objective was to establish closer ties with the Arab nations—especially with Libya, to which he himself headed a diplomatic mission and from which he hoped to obtain an influx of investments sufficient to restore prosperity and insure his remaining in power. This strategy was an absolute failure, but it did succeed in casting a chill on relations with the USSR and the rest of the socialist bloc.

Relations worsened as the Argentine domestic crisis prevented the development of any coherent foreign policy. The first attempted coup, led by ultrarightists in the armed forces, came in December 1975; although rejected by the rest of the military, it did lead the army commander in chief, General Jorge Videla, to announce that a coup would be inevitable if no political solution were forthcoming within the next ninety days. The political parties proved unable to produce a solution, and the armed forces, after rejecting Isabel Perón's offer to serve as a Uruguayan-style front for a military regime, overthrew the government on 24 March 1974 and installed General Jorge Videla as president.[18]

Soviet analysts closely followed the development of events and expected relations to deteriorate even further. The growing domestic crisis and the predominance of those sectors characterized since the end of 1974 as conducting an offensive against the progressive policies outlined by Perón, including the Peronist center-right and extreme right, the oligarchy and big business, paramilitary groups, imperialism, and the reaction in general, all pointed in this direction. According to these analyses, the counteroffensive had acquired a more vigorous and open character after Perón's death and was trying to unite all conservative and reactionary forces in order to create conditions favorable to a coup similar to the Chilean one of 1973.[19]

• The Military Government and Unexpected Rapprochement

When Isabel Perón's overthrow finally came, however, Soviet analysts avoided comparing it with the Pinochet coup. The new interpretation, which coincided with that of the PCA, tended to emphasize that the coup had been expected because of chaotic economic conditions and the wave of terrorism unleashed by ultrarightist and ultraleftist groups. Although unable to deny that military groups had attacked PCA headquarters and that Videla had described himself as "a devout Catholic of rigid opinions," Soviet commentaries noted that the new regime had promised to restore democratic rights and the republican system of government, and that the coup had been bloodless. The PCA noted that certain objectives of the new government coincided with the "vital interests of the people" and that the government had not adopted a Pinochet-style solution. In general, the Soviets and the PCA adopted a "wait and see" attitude, claiming that the armed forces included two groups: the *Pinochetistas* and those who favored a return to the constitutional system after "stabilizing the situation."[20]

The Argentine military regime, for its part, was extremely cautious in defining its future course of action, especially in foreign policy. The basic objectives outlined in the "Process of National Reorganization," issued on 24 March 1976, merely stated that the government would try to achieve a position in the Western and Christian world in accordance with the country's capacity for self-determination and vigorously reaffirmed the Argentine presence in the community of nations. Significantly, the document made no mention of Marxism or communism as responsible for the country's problems (as had occurred in 1966), stating only that national security would be enhanced by eradicating subversion and the causes that favored its existence.[21]

The military junta's Communique No. 32 detailed the posture the new government was to adopt in foreign policy: It would comply with the standards established by international law and strictly adhere to a policy of nonintervention in the internal affairs of other states, fulfill all its international obligations, maintain relations with all nations that respected international law, and strengthen cooperation and solidarity with nations with whom Argentina had historical and cultural ties and who shared the same values and objectives.[22]

The military junta closed Congress, suspended the activities of the political parties, removed the provincial governors and justices of the Supreme Court from their posts, placed the CGE and CGT (Confederación General de Trabajadores) under military control, and enacted a host of other measures aimed at controlling political life. On 26 March 1976 a law was decreed banning all political activity; that same day Communique No. 45 announced that a number of leftist parties and groups had been dissolved and their property and funds confiscated. Significantly, the PCA was not included and was allowed to keep its property; it was of course subject to the general ban on political activity imposed by law.[23]

On 3 April it was announced that the USSR had recognized the new government and on 6 April that Cuba had done likewise.[24] This seemed to confirm a general movement toward recognition of the new regime on the part of the socialist countries. The Cuban case was the most suggestive. Having initially granted the junta only conditional recognition, it soon fell in line behind the Soviet position and for the first time recognized a right-wing Latin American government with which it had deep political and ideological differences.[25]

Subsequent Soviet analyses of the Argentine military government were very cautious and tended to be based on the regime's declared objectives. Soviet reports noted the nonviolent character of the coup and the ambiguity of the new government's foreign policy.[26] The press also carried verbatim communiques issued by the PCA, which sought to explain the reasons for the coup and stated that the new regime would be judged by its actions.[27]

In August 1976 the Soviet magazine *New Times* carried an article that discussed the Argentine situation in great detail and noted that the errors committed by the Peronist government had created the worst crisis in the country's history.[28] The military was described as being surrounded by "working-class action, on the one hand, and reactionary attempts to set up a Chile-style dictatorship on the other." Although the article pointed out that the regime's economic policy was unpopular, it also noted that "Argentina's 'Pinochetistas,' who failed to achieve supremacy in the coup, are trying to impose their views": sharpened repression and forming an alliance with the United States to control the South Atlantic. Dividing the armed forces into two groups: "liberals"— antifascists in favor of collaboration with the political parties—and "ultrarightists"—whose "supreme goal [was] the destruction of communism . . . , repression of all democratic forces, and the establishment of a dictatorship," the article advocated "joint action by military and civilian patriots" to form a coalition government to rout Pinochetism and convert the armed forces into "an armed fist of the people in their struggle for firmer independence and national progress."

The rest of 1976 was largely uneventful in terms of bilateral relations, except for the minor incident involving a scuffle between Soviet technicians and Argentine citizens.[29] The most important step toward diplomatic rapprochement during this period was taken by the USSR and concerned the issue of human rights violations in Argentina. As reports of assassinations, torture, and disappearances increased, the military government found itself the target of vigorous criticism within the international community; pressures against Argentina mounted as some nations adopted punitive measures to express their disapproval.[30] Significantly, the pressures came chiefly from the United States and Western Europe, while the countries of the socialist bloc remained silent.

The Carter administration's decision to elevate the human rights issue to one of the central concerns of its foreign policy considerably worsened U.S.-Argentine relations. Attempts by Patricia Derian, assistant secretary for human rights and humanitarian affairs, to intervene on behalf of the politically persecuted aroused resentment in the Argentine military, who considered her demands inadmissible interference in Argentina's internal affairs. Relations reached their nadir in 1978 when the U.S. Department of State and the Export-Import Bank recommended denying Argentina loans because of its human rights violations[31] and the Kennedy-Humphrey amendment suspended military assistance.[32]

Initially, the USSR assumed a position of total indifference to Argentine human rights violations; they went unmentioned, much less denounced, by the Soviet government and press. But as criticism mounted and the Argentine case came to be discussed in international organizations the Soviets abandoned their position of neutrality and came to the defense of the Argentine government. At the beginning of 1977 it became evident that the USSR was maneuvering to block condemnation of the Argentine regime by the UN third commission (the human rights commission), which was meeting in Geneva.[33] Later, in March and August 1977, the Soviets voted against placing Argentina on the agenda of the UN human rights commission as a country to be investigated. On both occasions Argentina was excluded from the agenda by three votes to two, with the Soviet Union voting for exclusion and the United States in favor of initiating a formal investigation.[34]

The Soviet Union's position on Argentina becomes all the more significant when contrasted to its total support of UN reports condemning human rights violations in Chile and the propaganda campaigns in the Soviet media against Chile, and to a lesser extent, Uruguay. Soviet campaigns against Chile and Uruguay scarcely differed in substance from reports in the Western news media (they largely reported the same incidents); indeed, the only major difference was even harsher language of condemnation. Obviously, given these examples, one can see that the Soviet Union's special treatment of Argentina had little to do with the principle of nonintervention in internal affairs. Nor is it likely that its attitude was based on fear of inviting similar criticism. Attacks on Chile and Uruguay could just as easily be turned into a two-edged sword by suggesting uncomfortable comparisons between the treatment of political dissidents in those countries and in the USSR.

The most plausible explanation for the Soviet attitude toward Argentina is the distinctive characteristics of the relations between the two countries, both political and economic. In the economic sphere, the Soviets were determined to maintain excellent relations with Argentina after the coup and were little disposed to make moral gestures that would earn them the hostility of the junta and jeopardize trade. The Soviets' political analysis of the situation was equally cautious.

As illustrated by an article published in December 1977, Soviet analysts continued to believe that the armed forces harbored a moderate faction composed of "antifascists and liberals with democratic views," disposed to returning the country to constitutional government and who were headed by the "Two Vs," President Videla and the army commander in chief, Roberto Eduardo Viola.[35] This faction—according to the article—was confronted by another, a "minority, holding conservative views and speaking for the landowners, the stockbreeders, and the monopolists," whose power was concentrated in the navy and air force. According to this analysis, Videla's call for a dialogue to achieve national unity was favorably received by the trade unions and the political parties, including the PCA. The article attributed "political crimes"—human rights violations were not mentioned by name—to "death squads" who were not part of the government and ought to be suppressed by it, because their objective was to provoke a fascist putsch that would permit the installation of Chilean-type military government. The Videla government was regarded as having improved the political atmosphere, despite provocations from "ultras" on the right and the left, so that the trade unions and political parties could operate more openly despite the formal suspension of their activities. All this seems to indicate that the Soviets, along with the PCA, hoped that a definitive victory by the "liberal" sector in the army would result in a civilian-military coalition government disposed to maintain relations with the socialist countries even more cordial than those existing.

In September and October 1977, however, a diplomatic problem erupted when seven Soviet fishing vessels were captured by the Argentine navy, escorted to port, and accused of trespassing in Argentine territorial waters. The incident was handled with discretion by the foreign ministry, which merely sent a note of protest to the Soviet embassy.[36] Only Admiral Massera, the navy commander in chief took a hard-line stance, issuing public declarations describing the incident as a serious violation of Argentine sovereignty.[37] The Soviets insisted that the vessels had been outside the 200-mile limit and described the incident as a right-wing maneuver to "undermine the commercial, scientific, technical, and cultural ties" developed in recent years. The navy was described as an instrument of reactionary factions.[38]

It is likely that the navy actually was trying to jeopardize relations with the USSR; around the same time, the foreign minister, Admiral Montes, announced that he was holding talks with South Africa and other interested countries concerning the formation of a South Atlantic defense pact, which would obviously be directed against the Soviet Union.[39] Montes failed to receive the backing of the rest of the government, and the topic was dropped, for a time, by the government and press.[40] In what could be taken as a gesture of good will toward the USSR, several days later both governments announced that Soviet cooperation in the Middle Paraná project was in their mutual interest.[41]

During 1978 and 1979 relations between the two countries remained relatively cordial. One of the factors promoting this cordiality was Leopoldo Bravo's presence in Moscow as Argentine ambassador. Bravo, who had held the same post during Perón's first administration, seems to have concentrated on the economic side of relations, leaving aside ideological and political differences. In an article in *Convicción* in 1981, he declared that Argentina demonstrated its "independence by separating the political from the strictly economic," that "the Soviet Union is very careful concerning the internal affairs of countries with which it trades," and that "during those years [of his ambassadorship] they neither criticized, nor even mentioned, what we have been doing."[42] The last statement might be open to question, and should perhaps be taken as a diplomat's effort to speak kindly of his host country.

During 1978, and especially toward the end of that year, the Beagle Channel dispute between Argentina and Chile worsened, with both countries mobilizing troops. The Soviets largely ignored the situation, although some commentaries suggested that tensions were being fed by Great Britain and the United States, who were supposedly eager to exploit any conflict in order to appropriate oil and fishing reserves in the South Atlantic, gain control over the strait between the two oceans, and protect their interests in Antarctica.[43] Although the Soviets presented Argentine arguments in a favorable light and accused Britain of having used its role as arbitrator to exacerbate differences, they seemed to favor a peaceful solution, deferring to the position taken by the Communist parties of Argentina and Chile.[44]

Meanwhile, relations between Argentina and the United States continued to deteriorate, mainly over the human rights question. The Soviet Union, on the other hand, continued its silence and even helped Argentina in squelching criticism. At the 1979 Moscow Film Festival, a Swedish film relating the life of an Argentine political exile and critical of the military government drew protests from the Argentine embassy. The Soviets managed to have the film withdrawn, offering formal excuses and winning the gratitude of Argentine officials.[45] In another gesture of good will, the Soviet Union recognized the 200-nautical-mile economic zone, while the United States decided to challenge Argentina (as well as Burma and Libya) over the extension of the territorial limit beyond the traditional three miles.[46]

Argentine hostility toward the United States was evident at the meeting of the nonaligned nations in Havana in September 1979, where it voted for a Cuban resolution supporting Puerto Rican independence, demanding the withdrawal of U.S. bases from the Caribbean, praising the Sandinista revolution in Nicaragua, and condemning hostile actions by the United States against Cuba.[47] It is highly unlikely that Argentina's support for this resolution was due solely to its problems with the United States, however, for the resolution also included a clause supporting Argentina's reclamation of sovereignty over the Malvinas Islands (Falklands).

In September 1979, *New Times* published an article analyzing the Argentine situation in which Videla was described as a "moderate" who was combating "ultra-Right elements" trying to install a Pinochet-style dictatorship.[48] Stating that General Viola's role as army commander in chief "had created a more favourable situation for movement towards democratization," the article saw hope for a democratic agreement with the military that implied the "need to back the moderate circles in the armed forces in order to counter the ultra-Rights."

• From the Grain Embargo to the Malvinas Crisis

The Soviet invasion of Afghanistan and the subsequent grain embargo decreed by U.S. President Carter placed Argentina in a situation that, after some vacillation, resulted in strengthened diplomatic ties with Moscow.

On 10 January 1980, Argentina issued a communique announcing its refusal to participate in the grain embargo. It did condemn the invasion without mentioning the USSR by name, stating that "the world has been upset by the condemnable attitude of a power that has intervened with force in the internal affairs of another nation, with absolute contempt for any standard or principle."[49] Despite the harsh wording, the communique was much less effective than that issued at the time of the invasion of Czechoslovakia, in which the Onganía government had expressed its willingness to participate in any punitive measures taken against the USSR. On this occasion, however, the government justified its refusal to join the embargo by stating that it would not participate in sanctions adopted without its having been consulted and which emerged from decision centers outside the country. Argentina "has never been and will not be in the future an agent of foreign wishes or a last-minute subscriber to power strategies outside the international legal order."[50] The communique ended by stating that despite its opposition to economic sanctions, Argentina would attend the meeting called by the United States to discuss the embargo, even though it could not agree with unilateral measures and was unwilling to make sacrifices unless they were fully justified by legitimate national interests.

The last point suggested that the Argentine government was willing to strike a deal with the United States, bargaining its support for the embargo in return for cessation of pressures with regard to human rights, lifting the arms embargo, and issuing loans. If this was the Argentine strategy in Washington, it obviously failed, and the Argentine government repeated its decision not to join the embargo after the meeting.[51] However, it did vote in favor of a UN resolution condemning all intervention in Afghanistan and demanding the withdrawal of all foreign troops.[52]

Later efforts by Carter's special envoy, General Goodpaster, to convince the Argentine government to reverse its decision proved fruitless.[53] Goodpaster was unable to offer any of the guarantees Argentina demanded in return for joining the embargo, such as secure markets for Argentine grains, sales of nuclear material, an end to criticism of Argentina's human rights violations, lifting of the arms embargo, and the granting of loans. The only point to which Argentina agreed was not to exploit the international situation to its commercial advantage.[54] This promise was soon abandoned when Argentine grain prices rose considerably and Argentina moved to occupy the gap left by the United States in the Soviet market. The only sanction against the USSR finally adopted was the merely symbolic one of refusing to compete at the Moscow Olympics, but even this decision was reached reluctantly and with considerable delay.[55]

Immediately after Goodpaster's departure, a delegation from Export-Khleb, headed by Viktor Pershin, arrived in Buenos Aires to supervise the shipment of grain already purchased and to negotiate new contracts.[56] These efforts proved to be successful, since practically all the grain not already sold to other purchasers was bought by the Soviets.

Diplomatic relations grew more cordial during 1980. In May 1980 the Argentine foreign minister, Brigadier General Carlos W. Pastor, declared that relations with the USSR were "stable [and] productive" and "a powerful example of combining the 'pragmatic' with 'principles' — ideological and those of political philosophy — that every country has," because there is "a mutual respect in our relations that permits both sides to benefit from the flow of trade and technology."[57]

In July 1980 the secretary general of the Soviet foreign ministry, Yuri Fohin, visited Argentina; Soviet sources related that this type of visit assured the USSR's support for the election of the Argentine ambassador to the United Nations, Carlos Ortiz de Rosas, as secretary of the disarmament conference.[58] Issues discussed during Fohin's visit included possible Argentine support for a disarmament proposal to be presented by the Soviets to the UN General Assembly in September 1980, the supply of nuclear material to Argentina, and the feasibility of the USSR's supplying some of the turbines and generators for the Yaciretá power plant. Negotiators also discussed Soviet recognition of the García Meza regime in Bolivia, which was supported by Argentina but denied recognition by many Western governments because of its involvement in the international drug trade. The Soviet delegation agreed with the Argentine position of recognizing governments regardless of their origin and hinted that the Bolivian regime would be quickly recognized by Moscow.

Toward the end of 1980 the junta designated General Viola as Videla's successor in the presidency, for a term to begin on 29 March 1981. This decision was reached according to succession mechanisms worked out by the junta itself in 1976, and it at first presented no major internal problems. The decision was welcomed by the Soviets, who in numerous publications had already expressed their conviction that Viola was a moderate disposed to maintain good relations with the USSR. Soviet publications noted that he was "a professional soldier with a high-level military education" and had been "born to a family of Italian immigrants of modest means." He was considered to be "identified with the nationalist moderate wing of the armed forces" and "had declared himself for cooperation with all countries of the world, including the socialist, and especially the Soviet Union."[59]

Viola's presidency marked the beginning of a new orientation in domestic affairs, especially in economic policy, but his foreign policy reflected continuity in its attitude toward the USSR. Viola's minister of economics, Lorenzo Sigaut, was much less of an orthodox liberal than his predecessor, Martínez de Hoz. His plans called for the rebuilding of the country's productive apparatus, especially the industrial sector, which had been seriously debilitated in recent years. The last year of Videla's government had witnessed constant deterioration in the Argentine economy—declining GNP, inflation, banking crises, declining real wages, unemployment, and balance-of-payments problems—which required the adoption of drastic corrective measures. In the face of this disastrous scenario, the trade surplus with the USSR represented one of the few bright spots by helping to prevent an even greater deficit in the balance of trade and payments.

The new foreign minister, Oscar Camilión, was a lawyer and "developmentalist" politician who had been secretary of foreign relations under Frondizi and ambassador to Brazil since 1976. He was considered to be even more inclined than his predecessors to maintain friendly relations with the socialist and Third World countries. The Soviets reacted favorably to Camilión's appointment; in a short biography published in 1981 he was described—quoting an Argentine source—as a "defender of the principles of peaceful coexistence."[60]

By 1981 the amicable character of Argentine-Soviet relations had taken firm enough root to withstand substantial disagreement. In June-July 1981 the Eleventh Consultative Meeting on the Antarctic Treaty was held in Buenos Aires, at which time the Soviet delegate declared that his government was opposed to recognizing any nation's sovereignty over the Antarctic continent, and that despite the excellent relations between Argentina and the USSR, the Soviets made no exceptions.[61] Argentina, together with other countries, including Chile and Britain, claims sovereignty over part of Antarctica, including a large peninsula extending toward South America. Despite this difference, relations were unaffected, and the final resolutions approved at the meeting tended to confirm the maintenance of the status quo.

In July 1981 the Soviets announced that an Argentine cargo plane had illegally penetrated Soviet airspace, disregarded radio contact, and collided with a Soviet plane, plunging both of them to earth. The incident was shrouded in mystery; it was speculated that the plane was transporting arms from Israel to Iran, which was denied by both the Argentines and the Iranians.[62] Ambassador Bravo asked to inspect the site of the accident but was only granted permission to do so thirteen days after the crash. The incident was later brushed under the rug without much commentary from any of the parties involved, and the plane's mission and the circumstances of its crash have never been satisfactorily explained.

In August 1981 the United States sounded out the Argentine government on the possibility of sending troops to participate in the Sinai peacekeeping force. The invitation was received favorably by some elements in the military, principally because the Reagan government had lifted the arms embargo in May. The USSR, however, made no secret of its opposition to the proposal, stating that the "docile alignment" of the Latin American republics with the United States on this question contained considerable risks for the countries involved. Although some conservative elements regarded the Soviet statement as a threat, the foreign ministry issued no public comment. After lengthy negotiations, Argentina finally declined to participate in the peacekeeping force.[63]

A short time later, the Soviet Union again intervened on Argentina's behalf over the human rights issue. On this occasion the UN human rights commission had decided to consider as proven charges concerning "disappeared" persons when the state in question refused to cooperate with investigators. The vote was fifteen in favor to three against— Argentina, the USSR, and Rumania voting "no."[64] In this case the "no" vote favored Argentina more than the other two countries, since the case of "disappeared" persons was the principal cause of international pressure against the Argentine government.

The Argentine political situation changed considerably toward the end of 1981, for a number of reasons. The worsening economic situation, rising political and social discontent, dissension within the armed forces, and the illness of President Viola led the junta to request Viola's resignation. When Viola declined to comply, the junta decided to remove him from office; he was replaced on 22 December by the army commander in chief, General Leopoldo F. Galtieri.[65]

Galtieri initiated another shift in domestic policy. Most importantly, he capped a lid on the limited political opening begun under Viola and installed a neoliberal economic team in the economics ministry. The new foreign minister, Nicanor Costa Méndez, had already occupied that post under Onganía and had helped to elaborate and apply the doctrine of "ideological frontiers."

These changes in personnel seemed to indicate that relations with the Soviet Union would soon become chilly, especially since Galtieri and Costa Méndez appeared to be greatly interested in improving relations with the United States. Among the concrete steps they took in this direction were sending economic aid and military advisers to El Salvador and reviving the South Atlantic pact project. On the domestic front, Galtieri's hard-line policy against the political parties erased the possibility of creating a civilian-military coalition government, one of the projects favored by the PCA. Finally, the open-door policy proclaimed by the economics ministry threatened to perpetuate the pattern of selling products to the USSR and using the foreign exchange so obtained to make purchases in other countries, without balancing trade.

The USSR, however, displayed a friendly attitude toward the new government, and Brezhnev sent a message of congratulation to Galtieri in which he expressed the certainty that "the mutually beneficial relations established by the Soviet Union and the Argentine Republic will continue to develop for the good of both our countries and in accordance with our interests in strengthening world peace and international security." Gromyko sent a similar telegram to Costa Méndez.[66]

Despite the cordiality shown by the Soviets, conservative circles close to Costa Méndez began to discuss the possibility of withdrawing from the nonaligned movement, drawing the country closer to the United States, reopening talks on the South Atlantic pact with South Africa, aiding the Salvadoran government, and loosening ties with the USSR and the socialist bloc.

The government soon became openly critical of the Soviet Union. Costa Méndez declared that any action meant to dissuade the Soviet Union from invading Poland or interfering in Poland's internal affairs would be reviewed favorably by Argentina, and that the United States could count on Argentina's participation in a new grain embargo.[67] However, this idea was quickly rejected by other Argentine government sources, who emphasized that trade with the Soviets would continue uninterrupted and who criticized as "incoherent" the embargo on high technology decreed by the United States against Poland and the USSR.[68]

The Galtieri government issued the Salvadoran government credits, but it declined to provide military assistance. It is possible that some advisers were sent, as was speculated when Colonel Rafael Flores Lima, a member of the Salvadoran chiefs of staff, visited Buenos Aires in February 1982 and left with the promise of receiving Argentine assistance.[69] This policy apparently put a chill on relations with Cuba, which recalled its ambassador from Buenos Aires in January 1982; Argentina in turn recalled its ambassador from Havana in February.[70] That same month the Argentine ambassador was summoned home from Managua after the Nicaraguan foreign minister, Miguel D'Escoto, accused Argentina and Venezuela of plotting to overthrow the Sandinista government.[71] Faced with growing rumors of Argentine intervention in Central America, Galtieri was forced to declare that he would not send troops to any country in the region and that he was not inclined to review favorably any suggestions that he do so.[72] A short time later, however, Costa Méndez, on a visit to Brazil, declared that "if the East-West conflict spilled over onto American soil or constituted a threat to or attack on the peace or security of the hemisphere, Argentina could not stand aside," and would of course be on the side of the West.[73] The Soviets largely ignored Argentina's tilt toward the United States, even though the Soviet media devoted full coverage to the Salvadoran situation.

On 2 April 1982, Argentina used military force to occupy the Malvinas Islands (Falklands), sovereignty over which had been the subject of dispute ever since Britain took control of the islands in 1833. Within a few days the Argentine action had completely transformed the diplomatic picture. In a serious miscalculation, the military government seems to have counted on the benevolent neutrality—or even tacit support—of the United States, unconditional support from the Latin American countries and the Third World, lack of interest by the European countries, and a weak response from the United Kingdom.

The United States, however, openly sided with Britain after a brief attempt at mediation by Secretary of State Alexander Haig. Latin American and Third World support was strictly rhetorical, except perhaps for Cuba, Nicaragua, Panama, Peru, Venezuela, and Libya. The EEC imposed severe economic sanctions on Argentina from the opening days of the conflict. The UN Security Council strongly condemned the Argentine invasion and demanded the immediate withdrawal of troops. Great Britain sent a fleet and a large contingent of troops to recover the islands, and the conflict escalated into an undeclared war.[74]

The Argentine government, unexpectedly finding itself in confrontation with the developed Western world, was forced to seek diplomatic support from the Latin American, Third World, and socialist countries. The conflict, which the Argentines had originally presented as merely a territorial dispute between two countries, was now described as part of the larger anti-imperialist struggle between the developed North and the undeveloped South.

The Soviets gave strong, though merely verbal, support to the Argentine position. At the UN Security Council, the USSR abstained from voting on the resolution condemning Argentina, but did not use its veto. Although they supported decolonization, the Soviets did not wish to appear to be opposing a resolution which, in addition to demanding the withdrawal of troops, called for peaceful negotiations, since this could be interpreted as opposition to the use of peaceful means for resolving disputes.[75]

The Soviet ambassador to Argentina, Sergei Striganov, declared after a meeting at the foreign ministry that it was unacceptable for Great Britain to restore the islands' colonial status by using force. Meanwhile, Soviet publications criticized Britain for having violated UN resolutions on decolonization and endangering world peace and security. The United States was also harshly criticized, being accused of hypocrisy in its mediation efforts and of treachery in its ultimate support for Britain.[76]

Although it would be premature to draw any final conclusions, the Malvinas war has already had some tangible effects on Argentine-Soviet relations and on Argentine foreign policy in general.

First of all, the Anglo-Argentine conflict revealed the inefficacy of the Rio Treaty as a mechanism for resolving disputes between the

United States and Latin America, and it also became a source of tension between Latin American and the European countries. It is difficult to believe that relations between the developed capitalist countries and Argentina will overcome their frigidity for a long time. It seems likely that projects considered feasible not long ago, such as the South Atlantic defense pact, Argentine military assistance in Central America, and loosened ties with the socialist bloc, are now totally out of the question.

On the other hand, it is unlikely that Soviet support during the crisis will be quickly forgotten in Argentina, even though clearly the Soviets were acting in their own national interest by inserting the conflict into the global context of East-West rivalry. The lack of reliable allies among the Western nations has left Argentina with little choice but to draw closer to the socialist bloc and the Third World. If the need for reliable allies is added to the already substantial weight of advantageous trade relations, it seems highly probable the Argentine-Soviet relationship will become even closer than it was before. Furthermore, any future change of government in Argentina is unlikely to disrupt these relations; a civilian government would in all likelihood be ideologically attuned to rapprochement with the Soviets, while another military government would pursue a foreign policy not much different than that of the current regime.[77]

• Military Contacts

Argentine-Soviet military relations, in the sense of contacts between officers from the armed forces of both countries, began to develop in 1974 when the Gelbard mission visited the USSR. The Argentine delegation included officers from the army, navy, and air force, who held talks with their Soviet counterparts. Although official information is unavailable, these first contacts were probably a matter of mere protocol. They did open the way, however, for future visits and meetings, and were an important first step for the fiercely anticommunist Argentine military.

In November 1975 an Argentine delegation consisting of the pilots graduated that year from the Escuela Aeronautica Militar (air force academy) and headed by the academy's director, Brigadier General

I. Marquez, visited the USSR at the invitation of the Soviet defense ministry.[78] They were received by General A. Medvedev, chief of staff of the Soviet air force, and visited the aeronautical engineering academy and several air bases in Moscow area. Interestingly, at that time the Argentine air force was the most right-wing of the three armed forces, leaning in a conservative Catholic direction. In December 1975 a number of air force units headed by Brigadier General Capellini attempted a coup and used the occasion to issue anticommunist and ultrarightist declarations.[79]

According to the information available, during 1977 and 1978 military relations were uneventful. The only significant development was the posting of permanent military attachés in both countries' embassies charged with keeping open channels of communication.

The first military contacts of real consequence came in 1979, when the Soviet ambassador in Buenos Aires arranged for an exchange of visits by delegations headed by senior officers in each country's training corps.[80] A Soviet military delegation visited Argentina in August 1979; the head of the delegation, Lieutenant General Ivan Yacovich Braiko, and three colonels accompanying him were awarded the medal of the joint chiefs of staff in the presence of General Viola. TASS described the visit as a "transcendent event," and Braiko expressed hope that the visit would promote the development of fraternal ties between the Argentine and Soviet military training establishments. The Soviets offered to train Argentine troops in the Soviet Union, an offer Argentina agreed to study, and both countries agreed to assign a second military attaché to their respective embassies.

In September 1979 General José Montes, the Comandante de Institutos Militares (whose brother had been military attaché in Moscow shortly before), headed an Argentine mission to the USSR. The delegation visited a number of military schools in Leningrad, Moscow, and Kiev and received decorations from the Soviet authorities.[81] Montes met with officials from the Soviet defense ministry, probably discussing the exchange of military information, the possibility of arms purchases and sending Argentine personnel to receive training in the USSR.

Little is known about military contacts after this time, probably because some conservative Argentine circles were opposed to the visits.

However, it is likely that they continued, for the Argentines were interested in finding an alternative supplier of arms and training in case of continued tension with the United States, and the Soviets did not want to close a channel of communication that could provide future benefits.

During the 1978–80 period, Argentina and Chile were on the verge of war over the Beagle Channel dispute, and this situation, combined with the arms embargo imposed by the United States, increased Argentine interest in finding alternative arms suppliers. The problem was solved by turning to suppliers such as France, England, West Germany, and Israel, which offered the advantage of selling arms with which the Argentine military were familiar; in addition, these purchases were politically less dangerous than buying from the USSR. Although the Soviets were eager to reduce their trade deficit, they were probably also aware that arms sales to Argentina could be counterproductive by arousing suspicion and opposition among conservative groups and some of the military.

The Malvinas crisis could transform the Argentine-Soviet military relationship, which has been low-key. The EEC's economic blockade, U.S. aid to Great Britain, the Rio Treaty's failure to halt the British advance, and the realization that modern war required sophisticated weaponry available only in the developed capitalist or socialist countries could set the stage for closer military ties with the Soviet Union. For the moment, at least, no concrete steps have been taken and Soviet arms sales have not been forthcoming. However, it has been disclosed that Argentina received some Soviet weaponry included in the Libyan shipments that arrived during the Malvinas crisis. Reports that the Soviets aided Argentina by supplying satellite intelligence and helping to modernize radar systems during the crisis were denied, but the possibility that such assistance was provided remains open.

The principal problems with this military link are political and technical. From a political perspective, the Argentine military government remains anticommunist and fears that this type of rapprochement would constitute a decisive step that would destroy any chances of restoring good relations with the West. It is not prepared to take this step until it has exhausted all possibilities of reestablishing ties with its traditional suppliers of arms and training. From a technical perspective, the Argentine military is unfamiliar with Soviet equipment and would need a relatively long training period before they were familiar with its use. There are also problems with integrating Soviet arms into the Argentine arsenal, which is composed almost entirely of Western material. Moreover, fear exists that problems could arise in obtaining spare parts if political circumstances were to change; an additional disadvantage is that Soviet equipment is unavailable from other suppliers or through the clandestine international arms market.

However, if the Western countries maintain their arms embargo for a prolonged period of time, the Argentine military are likely to disregard these difficulties in order to reequip an arsenal severely depleted in the conflict with Britain. The air force would be the likeliest advocate of purchasing arms from the Soviets, since it suffered the greatest losses in the war and is incapable of producing aircraft equipped with sophisticated technology inside the country. The army, on the other hand, has its own armaments factories and would be inclined to purchase only high-technology items such as guided missiles or electronic defense systems. Finally, the navy was least affected in terms of losses and, like the army, would only be interested in purchasing missiles and other high-technology weapons and systems impossible to manufacture in Argentina.

• The Nuclear Question

Closely tied to the question of military, and especially strategic, cooperation is Soviet collaboration with Argentina in the nuclear field.

Of all the Latin American nations, Argentina has the most advanced nuclear technology, for both experimental and electricity-generating purposes. The country currently has one nuclear power plant in full operation, Atucha I, located in Buenos Aires Province; another, Embalse, in Córdoba Province, began to operate in 1983; and work has started on a third, Atucha II, next to Atucha I.

However, Argentina's failure to ratify the nuclear nonproliferation treaty has aroused fears, especially in the United States, that Argentina intends to develop nuclear weapons if it can acquire the personnel, technical expertise, and appropriate materials. The United States has thus refused to continue supplying Argentina with materials such as enriched uranium and heavy water required to expand the program.

As a result, Argentina has resorted to other suppliers, including West Germany and Canada, for the construction of reactors; a Swiss firm, Sulzner Brothers, is building a plant to produce heavy water. But these countries have come under pressure from the United States to discontinue their cooperation, making them potentially unreliable sources of material and technology, especially since the Malvinas crisis.

Argentina has thus looked to the Soviet Union for its purchases of heavy water. In 1981 the USSR shipped five tons of heavy water to Argentina, expressly stating that it would be used to resupply the Atucha I reactors and that the material was subject to the system of safeguards established by the International Atomic Energy Commission.[81] In early 1982 Argentina began shipping natural uranium for enrichment in the USSR.[82] On this occasion Vice Admiral Castro Madero, president of the National Atomic Energy Commission, declared that the shipment was made because of difficulties encountered in having the material enriched in the United States and that it consisted of approximately 100 kilograms to be used solely for production of radioisotopes; since the enrichment was only 20 percent, the uranium would be useless for producing nuclear weapons.

Argentine declarations on the peaceful aims of its nuclear program and the Soviets' extreme reluctance to assist in increasing the number of countries with nuclear weapons have not, however, quelled the fears of the United States and some countries bordering on Argentina. Indeed, the Malvinas crisis has heightened suspicion that Argentina intends to accelerate its nuclear program and construct nuclear weapons, which would be an effective means of dissuading and threatening real or potential enemies; at the same time creating a strategic imbalance in the Latin American area.

4 Manifest Consequences: Some Political and Social Effects

- The Partido Comunista Argentino and
  Argentine-Soviet Relations

Relations between the USSR and Argentina have not been limited solely to intergovernmental contacts; it is only to be expected that economic, diplomatic, and military relations should have an impact on Argentine society and politics. Perhaps the most outstanding political aspect is the role played the Partido Comunista Argentino (PCA) as Argentine-Soviet relations developed during the 1970s.

The PCA was founded in January 1918 under the name Partido Socialista Internacional and was the first Latin American communist party. Its creation was the result of a schism in the old Partido Socialista in which a group of members opposed to the pro-Allied position adopted by the leadership during World War I broke with the party after the Bolshevik victory in Russia. From the beginning, the PCA adopted a strongly pro-Soviet position, ever ready to defend all the strategic and tactical shifts proclaimed by the Communist party of the Soviet Union at the international level. As a result, the PCA was continually incapable of formulating policies appropriate to the domestic political environment and became increasingly isolated, especially from the workers and campesinos to whom its message was directed.

In 1920 the party accepted the twenty-one conditions of admission laid down the Communist International (Comintern), adhering to strict Leninist orthodoxy and adopting the name Partido Comunista Argentino. In later years there was a succession of internal struggles resulting in the expulsion of factions characterized as rightists (frontists), leftists (Bordiguistas and Trotskyists), and reformists (the Penelón group in 1927). The ultimate victors were the Stalinist faction headed by party leaders Vitorio Codovilla and Rodolfo Ghioldi. The PCA adopted the different positions propagandized by the Comintern, even though their appropriateness to Argentine circumstances was highly dubious. For example, when the Comintern was advocating cooperation between the Chinese Communist party and the Kuomintang, the PCA adopted a favorable attitude toward Yrigoyen's populist, Radical government, calling it progressive and anti-imperialist. However, when the Shanghai massacre produced an ultraleftist swing in the Comintern's positions, the PCA labeled Yrigoyenism as semifascist and openly opposed the government. Since Radicalism was a populist movement with democratic and nationalist overtones, characterizing it as fascist was totally incorrect, and opposition to it led to progressive isolation of the PCA from populist sectors without offering any political advantages in return.

In 1935, the PCA abandoned its ultraleftist stance (which had called for the immediate creation of a worker and campesino soviet state in Argentina and labeling Radicals and socialists fascists and social fascists), not because of domestic events, but because of the new line adopted at the Comintern's seventh congress. Held after the Nazi takeover in Germany, the congress endorsed the creation of popular fronts. The PCA immediately modified its political line and began to support the formation of a front consisting of Radicals, democratic progressives, and socialists, meanwhile applauding vigorously the "democratic" and pro-Allied views of governments such as that of President Ortiz. This strategy was maintained until the signing of the Hitler-Stalin pact, after which the PCA totally changed its position by defending "neutralism," defining World War II as an interimperialist conflict from which Argentina should stand aside, and promoting the creation of a national, anti-imperialist front (no longer "popular").

The German invasion of the USSR, of course, called for another about-face. The PCA became one of the most extreme pro-Allied groups and advocated the creation of a "democratic, national, antifascist front" designed to smash pro-Axis elements and to serve as a base of support for a government which would be allied with the Soviet Union, Britain, the United States, and other nations at war with Germany. At the same time, the party's program was reduced to emphasizing the necessity of supporting the Allied war effort; struggles for concrete gains by popular sectors were abandoned if they were considered to threaten shipments to countries like Britain. Meanwhile, the party's practical activity centered on raising funds for the USSR. The party attacked Castillo's conservative government and supported the Radical candidate, Alvear, who was considered strongly pro-Allied. The military coup of June 1943, resulting in the formation of an ultrarightist and neutralist government (some of whose members sympathized with the Axis), thrust the PCA into open opposition. It became one of the agitators for a front uniting all "democratic" parties—from conservatives to socialists—that would ultimately emerge as the Unión Democrática.

Sharp changes in position, political persecution, forced clandestinity, and the allegiance of much of the populace to the Radical and other parties made it impossible for the PCA to win any substantial support among the population. The emergence of Peronism in 1945 delivered the final blow to PCA aspirations of becoming a mass party with a large following in the working class and other popular sectors, the overwhelming majority of whom supported Perón. Neither its harsh criticism of the "corporative-fascist" character of Peronism nor its occasional attempts at rapprochement had any concrete result. The party was reduced to a small number of militants, most of them middle-class; the number of working-class cadres it was able to recruit was limited.

The fall of Perón in 1955 did nothing to change this situation, and the PCA continued to be a small party that, beyond its organizational capacity and ideological cohesion, had little to counterbalance the enormous weight of Peronism in the Argentine political arena. The problem of anticommunism among the Peronist masses was exacerbated by the PCA's tactical errors, such as its support of Frondizi in 1958, who later turned openly anticommunist; continued persecution; clandestine practices that hampered work among the masses; and factionalism, particularly in the 1960s as a result of the Sino-Soviet split and the attraction exercised by the Cuban Revolution.

From 1970 to 1973, the last years of the military government installed in 1966, the PCA was in open opposition. The *Revolución Argentina* government was energetically anticommunist and attempted to suppress all party activities, harassing its militants, closing its offices, and imposing anticommunist legislation. The PCA defined the military government as a "corporative-fascist [dictatorship] subservient to U.S. imperialism the landed proprietors, big capital and the reactionary forces," who used, during the Onganía and Levingston administrations, "the tactic of violence, terrorism and reaction all along the line."[1] The political liberalization begun by Lanusse and culminating in the 1973 elections was described as an "attempt to deceive the people" with the collaboration of Peronism, and Lanusse himself was called a "typical spokesman of the oligarchy enjoying the Pentagon's confidence.[2] The statute on political parties, which prohibited open electoral participation by the PCA, was considered a farce and a fascist regulation. Assuming a position more violent than its traditional one, the party called for a struggle to overthrow the dictatorship and install in its place a "new type of power that will proceed to effect the revolutionary changes the people demand."[3]

In 1972 the PCA continued its opposition and called for the creation of a national, democratic, anti-oligarchic and anti-imperialist front which would implement a democratic, agrarian, and anti-imperialist revolution.[4] At the same time, however, a political front, the Encuentro Nacional de los Argentinos (ENA), began to take shape; it would serve as a blind for the party and permit it to participate in the elections. The front was supposed to oppose the Peronist front, which was described as a tool of the bourgeoisie to forestall a truly popular revolution.[5]

The ENA, however, did not succeed as an alternative to the Peronists and Radicals, and so in 1973 the PCA ended up joining the Alianza Popular Revolucionaria, an electoral coalition formed by the Intransigente and Revolucionario Cristiano parties. This switch was justified by the progressive character of the coalition and the need to fight against the "election farce."[6] The PCA's participation in the alliance, which benefited from party's organizational and propagandistic capacities, allowed it to win two seats in the Chamber of Deputies.[7]

During this period the military government continued to enforce anticommunist legislation, blocking all possibility of legal activity by the party, although repressive measures eased somewhat in 1972–73 as the government devoted its attention to the more pressing struggle against Peronist and leftist guerrillas.

The Peronist victory made it possible for the PCA to resume legal

activity. The first measures adopted by the Cámpora government included amnesty for political prisoners (which freed a certain number of
communist militants), the repeal of repressive legislation (among them
the anticommunist law), and the voiding of the political party statute
decreed by Lanusse. The PCA subsequently altered its position on
Peronism, declaring that the elections had signified the rout of the
military dictatorship and that the party would "take a positive stand on
the new government," although it would "criticize every move injuring
the interests of the working class, the people and the nation."[8]

Among the positive measures supported by the PCA were domestic
policies (wage increases, nationalizations, repeal of repressive laws,
amnesty, and so forth) and foreign policy initiatives (recognition of
Cuba, North Korea, and East Germany and the adoption of a pluralist
foreign policy). The party stated that foreign policy "should be aligned
with the forces aspiring to an independent course in the interest of the
country, the struggle of the Latin American, Asian, and African peoples
for national liberation, and the great struggle for peace," and added that
it should promote "closer cultural relations with the Soviet Union and
other socialist countries."[9]

The democratic political relaxation allowed the PCA to abandon clandestine tactics and establish party locals, openly publish its periodicals,
participate without restriction in political life, and hold its first congress
since 1946. The fourteenth congress met in August 1973 and pledged
again the party's support for the progressive measures adopted by the
Peronist government, although it reserved the right to engage in "constructive criticism."[10] Speaking on foreign policy, Arnedo Alvarez—the
secretary general of the party—praised the government's plans to increase trade with the USSR, the end to the policy of ideological frontiers, and the recognition of Cuba and other socialist nations, but
criticized as false and dangerous the theory of the two imperialisms (the
United States and the USSR). He also called on the government to
denounce the Rio Treaty, withdraw from the OAS and help form a new
inter-American organization, express solidarity with the countries strug-
gling for liberation, and implement of an independent foreign policy.[11]

Despite previous attacks on Perón for his anticommunism, his profascist past, and the reactionary and bourgeois essence of Peronist doc-

trine, including Perón's theory of the two imperialisms, in 1973 the PCA began to offer him its support.[12] Given the PCA's criticism of Peronist domestic policy, especially after Cámpora's resignation, this support would seem to be based on the government's foreign policy, and especially on its quest for expanded economic ties with the socialist bloc. In September 1973 the PCA, for the first time in its history, offered its electoral support to Perón. And after the coup against Allende in Chile, the party called for "a united vigorous action of the masses [to dissuade] those advocating a coup . . . by completing the complicated and difficult process begun on 11 March that is directed against dependency [and] for national liberation." In the event of a coup, the party called for the creation of "popular resistance against the coup . . . on all fronts."[13]

The degree of support for the Peronist government paralleled the development of relations between Argentina and the Soviet Union. While Gelbard was minister of economics, "constructive" comments outnumbered "critical" ones in the PCA's declarations, but after Gelbard's removal and the subsequent freeze in relations with the Soviet Union, "critical" commentaries increased significantly. True, the death of Perón and the growing influence of López Rega, who was behind Gelbard's removal, led to a rightward shift in Argentine politics, but this evolution had begun long before with Cámpora's resignation and the ouster of the Peronist left from the cabinet. However, it was only after Gelbard's fall that the PCA began to suggest that reactionary elements were gaining the upper hand over the progressives in determining government policy.

Immediately after the death of Perón, the PCA called for the defense of the constitutional government of Isabel Perón against the offensive of the right and the danger of a coup or palace revolution.[14] But in September 1974—the month Gelbard was ousted—the party dropped its support for the Peronist government and called for the formation of a coalition cabinet including all democratic forces in view of critical situation of insecurity created by escalating terrorism and the government's equivocations and errors in judgment.[15]

During 1975 the PCA went into open opposition, calling the government's plans antipopular and antinational. It accused the government of moving increasingly to the right, abandoning its independent foreign policy, and moving closer to dictatorial regimes, such as the one in Chile. It also noted that "the government is violating its agreements with the countries of the socialist community while increasingly turning toward the United States."[16] After criticizing the reactionary policies of the economics ministers who succeeded Gelbard, the party called for mobilization of the masses to create a civilian-military government, but made no reference to the role—if any—Isabel Perón would play in it.[17]

This proposal to form a "civilian-military cabinet based on a broad democratic coalition," which implied the defenestration of the president and a de facto coup, was often repeated during this period. The party suggested that it was a better alternative than an open military coup in a situation in which "anti-communist and anti-Soviet propaganda are gaining ground . . . , with more and more attacks on agreements signed with socialist countries."[18]

However, when the coup finally occurred, the PCA's attitude toward the new government was favorable. A document published by the party after Isabel Perón's fall called the coup not the best solution to the crisis but said that the PCA would watch events as they developed and judge the regime by its actions. The document traced the causes of the coup to the serious situation created by the "reactionary supporters of López Rega and his protectress, María Estela Martínez" (dropping her married name, Perón, in a gesture of great symbolic value) and to the actions of members of the trade union bureaucracy, calling the deposed government "interim, incompetent, and corrupt."[19] In this same document the party supported the government's plan to combat corruption and subversion, and emphasized that the military had rejected a Pinochet-style solution. The new authorities were also asked to avoid persecuting Peronist workers and the political parties, enact domestic reforms, and develop a foreign policy without ideological discrimination.

The government's attitude toward the PCA stood in marked contrast to that of previous military governments. Immediately after the coup, the regime outlawed a wide range of leftist parties and groups, confiscated their funds and property, and began a wave of bloody repression against them.[20] At the same time, the activities of the rest of the traditional political parties, ranging from the right to the center-left, were only suspended. Interestingly, the PCA was the only leftist party spared banning and confiscation, although its activities were suspended along with those of the other "legal" parties. It was thus able to engage in thinly veiled activities, issue declarations, recruit new members, organize fund-raising campaigns, consolidate its internal unity, and establish relations with other groups that participated in the limited national political life.

However, the PCA was not totally immune to political repression and violence. Some militants disappeared, were assassinated or imprisoned; publications were occasionally banned; and local offices were attacked. For example, the building housing *Nuestra Palabra,* the official organ of the party, was attacked by an armed group in March 1976, and two persons were killed. However, a few days later the periodical *Tribuna Popular* appeared to take its place.[21] Even though these incidents were serious, it would have been surprising had the PCA escaped the repressive wave unscathed when victims included officials of the traditional parties, conservative journalists, moderate union members, and even diplomatic representatives of the military government, including the Argentine ambassador to Venezuela. What is important is that the party was not the target of an official policy aimed at extinguishing its existence, as were other leftist organizations. The attacks were the product of the "feudal" structure of the campaign of repression, in which each branch of the armed forces—and different groups within each branch—acted with complete autonomy, above all in the early months of the coup. Some of these groups were more anticommunist than others, and probably decided to direct their actions against the PCA. Nevertheless, the party survived this period with its internal structure and propagandistic capacity virtually intact.

The PCA was extremely cautious in criticizing the repressive policies of the military government; for example, at a time when political persecution was very severe (August 1976), the party protested against political terror by attributing it to "the hand of the criminals and the sinister activity of the imperialist CIA."[22] As a solution, it proposed that the government and the armed forces convoke a general assembly that would adopt the measures necessary to promote democracy and close the door to Pinochetism. Significantly, this statement was signed individually by party leaders and not by the central committee as such, an indication that the group was careful to observe the regime's norms concerning the suspension of political activity.

In its descriptions of the government, the PCA maintained that the armed forces included two groups: a moderate faction headed by Generals Videla and Viola; and a "Pinochetist" or hard-line faction whose leading members included, among others, Generals Menéndez, Vilas, and Suarez Mason. The former were regarded as favoring a gradual liberalization of the political process, while the latter were attempting its "fascistization." In line with this interpretation, the PCA issued a series of declarations that viewed the development of events optimistically: the moderates appeared to be consolidating their position, and the party called for the formation of a civilian-military coalition cabinet to guarantee the gradual return to democracy. The only vehement criticism was directed at the regime's domestic economic policy, which is understandable given its unpopularity among the population at large. But the party was very cautious in its comments on the human rights situation and the continued repression of political, trade union, and student groups.

During 1977 and 1978 the executive committee of the PCA (always signing as a group of individual communists) issued at least three declarations, on each occasion discussing statements or speeches made by General Videla. Constant themes were the need for: changes in domestic economic policy, elimination of the "Pinochetist" factions, a dialogue with political forces, an end to political crimes, the formation of a transitional government based on a civilian-military coalition, and the convocation of a constitutional assembly to establish new political institutions for the country.[23]

The secretary-general of the PCA, Gerónimo Arnedo Alvarez, picked up the same themes in 1979 when he recalled that the party's slogan was "renovated democracy or Pinochetism" and praised the positive role played by Videla and Viola in the march toward democratization. On the same occasion he said that the government's foreign policy "maintains a position of independence and good relations with all nations without regard to their political and economic structures and systems, [which is] significant because reactionary circles are exerting enormous pressures to convert us into satellites."[24]

Toward the end of 1979, Arnedo Alvarez repeated the party's position on the solution to the growing political and economic crisis, mentioning as minimum points of agreement respect for political liberties, freedom of the press and trade unions, and above all, changes in domestic economic policy that would allow the formation of coalition government.[25]

In 1980, the government's refusal to join the grain embargo against the USSR reinforced the PCA's tendency to give the government "critical support," putting it in the uncomfortable position of criticizing the regime's domestic economic policy while simultaneously applauding its foreign economic policy. A document issued by the PCA leadership in June 1980 said that Martínez de Hoz's economic policy was leading the country toward a major crisis, but also emphasized that "only one aspect of national economy has been protected from the generalized crisis, trade with the Soviet Union and the socialist countries."[26]

The secretary-general, Arnedo Alvarez, died in July 1981, and was replaced by Athos Fava, who let it known that this change in personnel would not affect the party's policy of critical support for the government. A pamphlet signed by the one of party's most important leaders, Fernando Nadra, discussed in detail the "progressive aspects" of the regime's foreign policy, including agreements and the high level of trade with the USSR, the refusal to join the grain embargo, active participation in the nonaligned movement, and the exchange of military missions with Moscow.[27] Referring to trade with the USSR, *Convicción* speculated that the PCA's enthusiasm was being reinforced by commissions on some contracts, and that it was possible that the party had initiated a direct dialogue with the government through Francisco Moyano, a presidential adviser.[28]

However, in the course of 1980 the domestic situation worsened considerably, making it impossible for the party to continue its moderate opposition to the government without running the risk of losing all popular support. Thus, in December 1980, Rubens Iscaro, a member of the central committee, characterized the dialogue promised by the government as "an attempt to win time," an attempt that has "degenerated into a monologue in which the government demands unconditional support for its policies."[29] Harshly criticizing the economic situation and political repression, Iscaro declared that only united action and the struggle of the proletariat could provide democracy, national independence, and social justice. Although he confirmed that the principal struggle was against imperialism and the oligarchy, and not against the military government, for the first time reference was made to the experience acquired by communists in countries ruled by fascist regimes. The pamphlet also dropped all mention of a civilian-military government, calling instead for an agreement with military groups in favor of forming a coalition government including all democratic forces.

Government reaction to the PCA's new hard-line position was swift. In February 1981 it shut down two of the party's publications, *Informe* and *Imagen de Nuestros Días,* which had been published without difficulty for years, but which the government suddenly discovered to be dedicated to "the dissemination of Marxism and promotion of class struggle," and thus a threat to public order and security. [30]

For a number of reasons, however, relations between the government and the PCA soon improved. Viola's assumption of the presidency led to a reversal of the Videla government's economic policy and the opening of a limited political dialogue; continued growth in relations with the USSR made it difficult for the party to remain openly hostile to the government; finally, the party feared new repressive measures if it continued its opposition.

In 1981 the PCA returned to its former position, claiming the 1976 military coup did not have a fascist character, that the alternative continued to be "renovated democracy or Pinochetism," and that the watchword was to "unite in consolidating the democratic forces with a view to speeding up the holding of a national democratic convention, the base for the formation of a civilian-military government representing all democratic forces"—a project that was opposed only by the "elitist and anticommunist right [that] blocks full dialogue between the government and the democratic forces." [31]

Later in 1981, Athos Fava stated that "after five difficult and hard years, the facts confirm the correctness of the unified and active line established by the communists . . . directed at promoting united grassroots action, building and combining forces [that] direct their fire at the main enemy, fascism in its Pinochetist variant . . . , [and] differentiating and separating the diverse sectors of the heterogeneous group in power."[32] In the same article, Fava noted that "despite the pressures of Yankee imperialism and those sectors most compromised by it, Argentina continues to develop its relations with the socialist countries, especially the USSR," noting that bonds are being established in cultural and artistic affairs and sports, with great impact among the masses." Referring to Argentina's refusal to participate in the grain embargo and the signing of trade agreements, Fava concluded by saying "Argentine-Soviet relations are not a temporary arrangement: they are evolving and have a firm foundation."

In September 1981, in an interview given in Hungary, Fava declared that the provocations of the ultraleft had given the junta the opportunity to shut down democratic and worker organizations, but it had not done so.[33] He added that "the failure of fascism to win in Argentina as it did in Chile is due to continual conflicts within the army [between] the liberal wing and those we call Pinochetists," and that "the communists, together with other democratic forces . . . support the liberal wing against the Pinochetists." Fava called the election of the "liberal" Viola as president "no small thing," even though his government served the interests of the bourgeoisie. Viola was praised for having rejected the U.S. plan for a South Atlantic defense pact, for its reluctance to send troops to the Sinai, for opposing South Africa's racist policies, and for recognizing the rights of the Palestinians and the Namibian independence movement. Finally, the junta was described as upholding Argentina's national interest against Washington in its foreign economic policy.

Given these declarations, it is obvious that Viola's replacement by General Galtieri in December 1981 was not welcomed by the PCA, all the more so when Galtieri appointed new ministers of economics (Juan Aleman) and foreign relations (Nicanor Costa Méndez) who seemed likely to revert to the policies of their predecessors. Aleman did in fact adopt an orthodox liberal economic policy that equaled or even superseded that developed by Martínez de Hoz, while Costa Méndez sought to strengthen ties with the United States and loosen those with the socialist countries and the Third World.

However, the PCA was not forced into opposition by these changes.

Before any of the policy shifts could take firm root, the Malvinas crisis intervened and changed the political situation completely.

The party, along with the USSR and the rest of the socialist countries, immediately realized the new possibilities opened by the crisis for achieving a total realignment of Argentine foreign policy and effecting changes in domestic politics more in tune with communist objectives. On the other hand, the PCA had long been a supporter of regaining Argentine sovereignty over the Malvinas. During the Videla presidency, the party had declared that "in the recuperation of national sovereignty over the Islas Malvinas . . . the government of President Videla can count on the support of public opinion." The party also called for "deeds" and insisted the islands be returned to Argentina "without conditions."[34]

It is thus not surprising that the party strongly supported the position of the military government once the crisis began. The secretary general, Athos Fava, traveled to Moscow and from there stated that "the successes of 2 April (the date the islands were occupied) have great national importance and international implications, and they will take their place in Argentine history regardless of who achieved them or the special circumstances under which they took place."[35] Fava defined the conflict with Britain as "an anti-imperialist and anticolonialist struggle" that had been undertaken to prevent the establishment of foreign military bases on Argentine territory and to put an end to the indiscriminate extraction of the country's natural resources. After criticizing the U.S. position and the European economic sanctions against Argentina, Fava declared that "a realistic way of overcoming this situation would be to increase trade . . . with the Soviet Union, [because] we believe economic relations with the USSR have been developing well in recent years and have a brilliant future." Fava used his stay in Moscow to discuss the Argentine-British conflict with high Soviet officials, including Boris Ponomarev, secretary of the Central Committee of the PCSU, and Karen Brutants, chief of the international department of the Central Committee.

Meanwhile, in Argentina, the rapid development of events had forced the government to loosen political controls and allow massive public demonstrations, in which the PCA actively participated. The party also used the opportunity to establish closer contacts with other political groups and members of the government.

All this indicates that as long as relations between Argentina and the Soviet Union remain cordial, the PCA will continue to support the government, or its successors, on most policies, restricting its criticism to specific domestic issues such as economic policy. The party is likely to continue avoiding open confrontation with the government *en bloc*, differentiating between factions with whom it desires to maintain good relations and others it considers convenient to criticize.

• Social Consequences of Relations with the Soviet Union

Relations with the Soviet Union have affected Argentine society in ways that deserve study. Growing trade and the diversity of economic ties have created powerful interests within important socioeconomic sectors determined to preserve, and if possible, to expand bilateral relations. For the first time in many years, agricultural producers and marketing organizations have found a secure export market that guarantees a certain stability of demand over the medium term and pays prices corresponding to those prevailing on the international meat and grain markets. This is of extreme importance to the agricultural sector, because its traditional customers do not provide similar guarantees and, in recent years, have tended to reduce their level of purchases or to buy in widely fluctuating quantities from year to year.

The EEC countries, traditionally the most important market for Argentine exports, have for some time reduced or stabilized their purchases. Sanitary regulations and self-sufficiency in meat production, protectionist measures, and purchases made in other parts of the world have all contributed to the decline in Argentine exports.[36]

The Latin American nations constitute important markets because of their proximity to Argentina and their need to import meat and grain, but periodic balance-of-payments crises force them to apply import quotas. The consequent negative effect on the volume and stability of demand for Argentine products is indicated by the yearly fluctuations in export figures for exports from Argentina to the LAFTA countries.[37] The Arab countries, which have the foreign exchange to import large quantities of foodstuffs, do not have sizeable populations; Argentine exports to those countries have thus remained at a low level.[38] Most of the other Third World countries do not have the foreign reserves to import large quantities of meat and grain, even if they wanted to, and thus account for an extremely small proportion of Argentina's foreign trade.[39] Finally, countries like the United States, Canada, Australia, and New Zealand are competitors with Argentina. They do not import Argentine agricultural products, or only sporadically and in small quantities. What is more, their products are directed at the same markets as Argentina's, often with the advantage of lower shipping costs owing to their greater proximity to large importers.

The Soviet Union's emergence as the largest individual purchaser of grains in the international market has had a destabilizing effect on prices, which now depend largely on the volume of Soviet purchases; these are in turn closely related to climatic factors and the vagaries of Soviet agricultural policy. The 1980 grain embargo prompted the Soviets to diversify as much as possible the sources of its imports, and it is clear that in the future they will try to avoid depending on the United States for the largest share of imports.[40]

These two factors, production problems in the USSR and the desire to circumvent the (at times) politically motivated export policies of the United States, have had a highly positive effect on Argentine producers, guaranteeing them both minimum purchase contracts over the medium term and higher prices for their exports. Specifically, fixing prices of products sold to the USSR to those prevailing on the international market has allowed Argentina to discontinue offering discounts in FOB prices—a strategy necessary to make its products competitive with those of countries enjoying lower shipping costs.

Argentina has faced difficulties on several fronts in the case of meat exports. The Common Market had enormously reduced its meat imports (by more than 50 percent between 1978 and 1980), and had also begun to "dump" its own surplus production in markets such as Poland, Egypt, and Greece—a policy described in Argentina as: "They won't buy from us, and they won't let us sell."[41] To these must be added specifically Argentine problems such as outbreaks of hoof-and-mouth disease, higher shipping costs, the closing of large companies producing canned and processed meats, and occasional revaluations of the peso, all of which helped to close certain markets and stimulate competition from marginal producers, including Brazil and South Africa. All this underlines the importance to Argentine producers of agreements reached with the Soviet Union which, in addition to circumventing the problems outlined above, diminish the influence of middlemen and often guarantee prices higher than those received by other exporting countries in the international market (as happened, for example, with the meat sold to the Soviets).[42]

Not surprisingly, representatives of agricultural producers and marketing organizations have expressed satisfaction with trade with the Soviets, including traditional organizations such as the Sociedad Rural Argentina, the Cámara Argentina de Frigoríficos Industriales y Exportadores de Carne, CARBAP, and the Bolsa de Cereales de Buenos Aires, as well as officials in the ministries of economics, agriculture, and commerce.[43] This sector, which has historically been anticommunist and anti-Soviet and opposed to leftist measures such as agrarian reform and the nationalization of foreign trade, has obviously decided to distinguish between economic rapproachement with the USSR, which it favors, and conciliation with domestic pro-Soviet sectors, which it openly opposes. However, its situation is not an easy one, since the growing dependence on Soviet purchases imposes limits on attacks on "communism" that might lead the government to reestablish "ideological frontiers" and abandon the relaxation of tensions with the USSR. These contradictions were revealed at the time of the grain embargo, when these sectors, despite their ideological sympathy for the boycott, acted in their own economic interests by refusing to join. None of this suggests, of course, that these groups now consider themselves outside what they call the "Christian and Western world," but it is evident that without access to alternative export markets, economic interests will take precedence over political sympathies.

The existence of interests favoring relations with the USSR is less manifest in the Argentine industrial sector, mainly because the Soviets are more interested in buying primary products than manufactured goods. An additional factor is that the neoliberal economic policy of recent years has hit Argentine industry hard, forcing out of business many companies that used to export their goods, or making the prices of Argentine goods uncompetitive on the international market.[44] There do exist, however, some industrial sectors interested in forming joint enterprises with the Soviets in order to import machinery at reasonable prices and to obtain new technology and favorable financing conditions. To date, only one joint enterprise has been established, between Ingeniería Tauro and Energomashexport; the formation of similar enterprises in the fields of metallurgy, fishing, coal, and oil are under study.

Argentine industrial firms are also interested in purchasing Soviet machinery and equipment at reasonable prices and with very favorable financing conditions; some metallurgical firms have already made such purchases.

The importance of the industrial sector could increase if government economic policy returns to protectionism and promoting industrialization. In this case, the government would come under pressure from industry to maintain good relations with the Soviet Union in order to guarantee supplies of spare parts, obtain technical assistance, and assure maintenance of equipment already installed.

On the other hand, those industries that have survived the economic crisis look to the Soviet Union as a potential market for their products, and are likely to pressure future governments to reach agreements specifying increased Soviet purchases of manufactures. Markets lost in other Latin American countries in recent years—markets which would be difficult to recapture even with a change in government economic policy—make the Soviet Union an even more attractive and necessary market for Argentine industry.

State-owned enterprises are another powerful interest group favoring continuity in relations with the Soviet Union. These state-owned companies are active in raw materials extraction and processing (Yacimientos Petrolíferos Fiscales, Yacimientos Carboníferos Fiscales), energy (Agua y Energía Eléctrica, SEGBA), metallurgy (SOMISA, Fabricaciones Militares), transportation (Aerolíneas Argentinas, Ferrocarriles Argentinos, ELMA), telecommunications (ENTEL), and chemicals (ATANOR), and carry considerable weight in the Argentine economy. Some of them, including Agua y Energía Eléctrica, SEGBA, YPF, and YCF, have been the chief purchasers of Soviet equipment and machinery in recent years, and several have signed contracts with the Soviets for the supply of new products. It is thus reasonable to assume that the state-owned sector includes numerous partisans of continued relations with the Soviet Union, whose reasons include relying on diverse markets for the purchase of capital goods, the advantageous prices and financing conditions offered by the Soviets, the availability of new technology, and the desire to "buy from those who buy from us."

As with privately owned companies, those state-owned enterprises that already own Soviet equipment are concerned to guarantee themselves an adequate supply of spare parts, technical assistance, and after-sales maintenance. Companies engaged in the production of nuclear energy are especially interested in continued relations with the Soviet Union, which has become their chief supplier ever since the United States placed a quasi-embargo on providing Argentina with nuclear material. Such companies are convinced that a deterioration in bilateral relations would close access to one of the few sources of advanced nuclear technology available to the country.

A fourth group with an interest in continued ties with the Soviets are producers of regional specialties (wine growers in Mendoza and San Juan, sugar producers in the north, fruit growers in Río Negro and Mendoza, wool producers in Patagonia, and so on). In recent years they have suffered greatly from the contraction of the domestic market, the impossibility of placing their products on the international market at competitive prices, and neoliberal economic policy in general. Clear evidence of these groups' interest in the Soviet connection was provided in the meetings between the Soviet trade delegation and producers and provincial authorities in Mendoza and San Juan in 1981.[45]

All these socioeconomic groups are acutely aware that the export sector has always been one of the weak points in the country's economic structure. The export sector earns most of the foreign exchange required to cover costs for essential imports, pay the external debt, maintain an adequate level of reserves, and achieve a balance of payments. If the export sector enters a crisis, the entire economy is disrupted, leading to unemployment, lower wages, economy is disrupted, leading to unemployment, lower wages, high interest rates, reduced production, and, finally, generalized recession. It is thus readily understandable that all sectors of the Argentine economy, whether directly involved in foreign trade or not, support the expansion of trade with the Soviet Union, especially in light of the fact that Argentina, as in 1980, habitually experiences a trade deficit with all other nations and regions of the world.[46]

Obviously, some of the groups mentioned above have had and continue to have influence with and within the government. Specifically, certain agricultural producers, financial and industrial organizations, and the heads of the state-owned enterprises have directly participated in drafting the policies implemented by the Argentine government. This direct influence reached its peak during Viola's presidency, when he "corporatized" the economics ministry, awarding the agriculture portfolio to Jorge Aguado, a representative of the powerful agricultural interests of Buenos Aires Province, CARBAP, and the industry portfolio to Guillermo Oxenford, a director of UIA, one of the largest industrial organizations. This practice allowed the respective interest groups to exercise an unmediated influence on Argentina's national and international economic policy. Since the end result of these policies was an unprecedented expansion of ties with the Soviet Union, it appears that economic considerations far outweighed any political or ideological antipathies.

The Malvinas crisis, with its far-reaching impact on all aspects of national life, also reinforced the tendency to improved relations with the Soviet Union. The crisis not only revealed the fragility of friendly ties to the United States and Western Europe, but also generated fierce resentment among the population at large against the West, allowing certain sectors to express more openly their sympathy for the USSR and the socialist bloc in their double roles as customers and diplomatic allies.

In conclusion, it seems likely that the social and economic pressures favoring closer ties with the USSR will continue for some time to come. Based on the objective interests of important sectors of the Argentine population, these pressures would ease only in response to significant changes on the domestic and international levels. Relations with the Soviet Union have gone beyond being a temporary matter of convenience, and any future government, civilian or military, is unlikely to disrupt them in view of the economic, political, and social problems such a policy would create.

For its part, the Soviet Union appreciates that the existing situation and the need and/or desire of various social sectors to continue strengthening bilateral ties represent progress in achieving its long-term goals, although the process is difficult and complicated. These goals have been relatively clear ever since relations were initiated. The USSR has always been interested in establishing and maintaining a diplomatic presence in Latin America, especially in the region's most important countries, including Argentina, Brazil, and Mexico. While official recognition by the maximum possible number of countries adds to Soviet stature as a world power, the Soviets also seek to develop contacts in order to obtain information on the region and eventually play an influential role within it. From the economic point of view, the primary goal has been to establish mutually beneficial trading relations by importing those products—especially agricultural—which the USSR does not produce in sufficient quantity to satisfy internal demand and by exporting Soviet goods to reduce its trade deficit.

For a long period of time, however, Soviet policy toward Latin America in general, and toward Argentina in particular, was shackled to Stalinist conceptions of a world divided into two openly hostile blocs, the socialist and capitalist. Only after the death of Stalin and the Twentieth Congress of the CPSU did the Soviet leadership replace this simplistic formulation with a foreign policy designed to seek closer ties with the nations of the Third World, including Argentina. The old Stalinist line of irreconcilable division, of struggle to the end, was replaced by a more flexible formulation. The world was now divided into a "peace zone" formed by the USSR, the socialist nations, and the Third World, and the group of advanced capitalist nations, with which it was possible to coexist peacefully. A corollary of this post-Stalinist vision was the development of diplomatic, economic, and cultural relations with the nonaligned nations, of which those outside the pro-Western camp were to be considered real or potential allies of the Soviet Union.[47]

Accordingly, the Latin American nations, which Stalin in 1951 had considered among the most aggressively anti-Soviet members of the United Nations (along with the NATO countries)—puppets of American imperialism eager to win economic advantage from conflicts in Europe or Asia[48]—were viewed in a totally different perspective by the new Soviet leaders. In 1956 Nikolai Bulganin, the Soviet premier, announced that the USSR was willing to develop ties with the Latin American nations on the basis of peaceful coexistence, friendly cooperation, noninterference in internal affairs, and mutually beneficial trade relations.[49] Subsequent changes in the Soviet leadership did not affect the new foreign policy. The Soviets consistently displayed open interest in establishing diplomatic relations with the majority of Latin American nations and placed greater emphasis on developing trade.

The fundamental objectives of Soviet foreign policy can be easily listed: to assure a diplomatic, economic, and cultural presence appropriate to the USSR's stature as a superpower with global interests to be preserved and protected; to establish economic relations that are both economically and politically profitable; to facilitate and promote tendencies toward nonalignment in Latin American foreign policy that would weaken links with the United States and other developed capitalist nations; and, finally, to be in a position to assist friendly governments and political movements without generating hostility from governments threatened by those movements and without incurring great expense in support of sympathetic regimes. The Soviet strategy for achieving these goals can justifiably be called pragmatic, for it seeks to obtain diplomatic, economic, political, and military benefits from normal relations between states without running the risk of provoking hostile reactions. Since it is highly improbable that the Argentine political situation will change drastically—for example, that an openly revolutionary situation will develop, or that a hard-line anti-Soviet government will take power—the Soviet Union has little reason to alter its pragmatic policy toward Argentina. Everything seems to indicate that the present characteristics of Soviet rapprochement with Argentina will continue indefinitely, since they assure the USSR the greatest benefits at a very low diplomatic, political, and economic cost.

5 Conclusion: Shared Interests

• The Economic Foundation

Relations between Argentina and the Soviet Union have been based on their complementary productive sectors and their respective import and export needs. From the beginning, the relationship between the two nations has been built on economic interests, specifically trade. Even as other bilateral ties have developed in recent years, trade has remained central, with the Soviet Union emerging as the largest single purchaser of Argentine exports.

Argentine interest in these relations resides in the country's role as a major exporter of meat and grains. The ranches and farms of the pampas enjoy a number of comparative advantages that allow them to produce and export at relatively low cost, and small capital investment results in large foreign exchange earnings. This "cheap" foreign currency earned by the agricultural sector plays a key role in the Argentine economy, since it—at times—permits a positive trade balance and provides the economic space necessary for the development of industrial, commercial, and service activities. Accordingly, problems with obtaining adequate prices for agricultural products on the international market disrupt the economy as a whole by breaking one of the essential pieces in the economic chain.

All sectors of the Argentine economy thus pay keen attention to developments in the international market for meat and grains that could affect prices and sales volume. In recent years, trade barriers erected by traditional customers and increased competition from other producer-nations have led to abrupt fluctuations in demand and price levels, making the Argentine search for alternative customers all the more urgent. Argentina's difficulties have been compounded by its great distance to the major European markets and resulting higher shipping costs; the erection of trade barriers and the export of subsidized meat by the Common Market; and the general state of the world economy, especially since the 1973 oil crisis, which has led most nations to reduce their import quotas.

In the face of such problems, the USSR constitutes a potential alternative customer of enormous importance. Food production and distribution have always been one of the notorious weak points of the Soviet economy. Successive shifts in agricultural policy since the October Revolution, including "war communism," the New Economic Policy (NEP), forced collectivization under Stalin, and Khrushchev's attempt to introduce incentives and expand cultivation in western Siberia, have all been counterproductive or brought meager success. The inefficiency of the collective farms, the lack of adequate incentives, the poor transportation system, and simple bad weather result in consistently low production.

Several sociopolitical factors affecting agricultural policy make the Soviets' problems even more acute. For a large part of the adult Soviet population, fears of a severe food shortage are fueled by their personal experiences with hunger during the famines of the 1930s and World War II. The government has been responsive to these fears and adopted policies such as freezing bread prices and trying to avoid shortages of other foodstuffs. It seems very likely that caution in this regard has been heightened by outbreaks of popular discontent against price increases, such as those that occurred in Novosibirsk in 1962 or in Poland in 1970.

Another important element was the policy decision to cover grain production deficits, especially after 1972, by resorting to massive imports. This decision was reached after weighing two alternatives: restriction of domestic consumption or buying abroad. The first option was considered more dangerous than the problems that would arise from the loss of foreign exchange and gold due to importing. Once it was reached, the Soviets stuck to their decision, even though in some years poor harvests and supply contracts with Cuba, North Vietnam, Egypt, and some Eastern European nations obliged them to make huge grain purchases in the United States and other exporting countries.

None of this, however, necessitated economic rapprochement between the USSR and Argentina, since purchases from international trading companies in the United States, Australia, and Canada fully covered Soviet demand. Only in 1980, when the U.S. grain embargo created a shortage, did the Soviets realize the vulnerability of their position in relying on suppliers who subjected their sales to political preconditions, such as the withdrawal of Soviet troops from Afghanistan. It was at this moment, when Argentina refused to join the boycott for its own economic and political reasons, that both countries came to view each other as relatively safe and stable trading partners. Expanded relations were thus not limited to the special circumstances of 1980, but were soon fixed in the signing of medium-term agreements for the placement of Argentine meat and grain on the Soviet market.

This situation offers advantages to both parties in that it assures Argentina a market for a large part of its exportable surplus and the Soviet Union a steady supply of part of its import requirements. Some problems do exist, though. For the Soviets, the major problem is the profound imbalance of trade, which represents a significant drain on its hard currency reserves. For Argentina, the major problem is the excessive concentration of sales in the hands of a single purchaser, and the attendant danger that the country could become as dependent on the Soviet Union as it was on Great Britain before World War II. The country would also face enormous difficulties should the Soviets decide to reduce or suspend their purchases.

The complementary needs of both countries are also expressed, although less dramatically, in Argentina's plans to expand its infrastructure, especially hydroelectric projects. Although various sources of equipment, technology, and assistance are available, the USSR offers a number of advantages, including its low bids, favorable financing terms, and experience with rivers with moderate grades. And of course the Soviets are interested in reducing their trade deficit through such collaboration. Problems such as unfamiliarity with Soviet technology, adequate supplies of spare parts and after-sales maintenance, disagreements on interpreting contracts, and doubts concerning the quality of the equipment have largely disappeared as more and larger purchases are made. Other problems, such as the government stalling on purchases because of balance-of-payments problems and the disinclination of the private sector to buy Soviet, have not been resolved. However, both governments have recently seemed to agree on the necessity of increased purchases by Argentine state-owned enterprises, and their managers have come under pressure to participate more actively in increasing imports from the USSR.

It thus seems likely that economic relations between the two nations will continue to expand and diversify in the near future, especially since diplomatic, military, and social developments are working to mutually reinforce closer ties in all areas. It would be very difficult for Argentina to sever or reduce its ties, given the present impossibility of finding alternative customers of comparable stability. Neither is it likely that the USSR will abandon Argentina in favor of suppliers whose sales are subject to political and diplomatic preconditions.

Both countries, however, might well try to modify certain aspects of their present relationship. Argentina could try to diversify its export markets in order to prevent excessive dependence on a single purchaser. Any such attempt, however, would meet with the difficulties already mentioned, such as hard-currency shortages in the Third World, trade barriers in Europe, small markets in the Arab countries, and competition from the United States, Australia, and Canada.

The USSR might try to modify the basic trade pattern by increasing its exports to Argentina, or by changing the terms of payment to providing Argentina with credits for the purchase of Soviet goods or requiring the direct exchange of products. The first approach requires the good will of the Argentine government, and could run into difficulties because of continued balance-of-payments problems and the reluctance of the Argentine private sector to buy Soviet goods. The second approach would be even more difficult to implement, since Argentina relies on the currency derived from Soviet trade both to keep the economy functioning and to begin to pay off its enormous external debt, which now amounts to more than US$40 billion. The most likely course of events is that Argentina will increase its imports from the USSR by reducing its imports from the West, while the Soviets will develop a more dynamic and aggressive export policy for the Argentine market, perhaps employing some of the "marketing" strategies successfully used by Western companies.

• Rapprochement and Rejection

The cycles of rapprochement and rejection in Argentine-Soviet relations have been fundamentally determined by the attitudes of Argentine governments since 1917—attitudes themselves determined by a combination of domestic and international factors.

On the domestic political level, it is apparent that before 1976 reformist and populist constitutional governments (the presidencies of Yrigoyen, Frondizi, Illia, and Perón) attempted to strengthen ties with the Soviet Union, especially commercial ties. The ideologies of all these governments, whether Radical or Peronist, favored development and an independent foreign policy. Why they were unable to achieve their goals is a topic beyond the scope of this book, but all attempted to promote trade and establish relations with all countries of the world. This strategy was meant to reduce Argentine dependence on the Western powers and to gain Argentina the leadership of Latin America.

The implementation of this type of foreign policy by reformist governments, however, met with a number of obstacles. First, many of these governments were from the beginning or came to be in the course of their existence extremely weak and unstable, and were thus unable to resist pressures from civilian and military conservatives against closer ties with the socialist countries. Without strong opposition they tended to maintain cordial relations with the USSR and the socialist bloc, but once orchestrated campaigns by diverse pressure groups became sufficiently strong, they preferred to retreat and protect a political flank exposed to attacks that could endanger their stability. Moreover, this tactical step was facilitated by the fact that both Peronists and Radicals were nationalists opposed to foreign influences, which included communism as the supposed agent of the Soviet Union. The rejection of communism, and by extension of the USSR, was an always latent tendency that rose to the surface when it proved necessary to justify freezing relations without admitting a concession to domestic or foreign pressure.

Conservative civilian governments and military regimes before 1976 were decidedly anticommunist and anti-Soviet, and generally unconcerned with political independence and economic autonomy of a type that would have led to contacts with the Soviet Union. On the contrary, they refused recognition or maintained relations at the lowest possible level, often verbally attacking the Soviet Union both at home and abroad.

The international situation has also affected the evolution of Argentine-Soviet relations, although the direction of internal and international developments have not always coincided. In some cases, such as in the periods 1930–41, 1955–58, and 1966–70, situations such as the international isolation of the USSR, the cold war, and East-West tensions have been contemporaneous with anti-Soviet governments in Argentina, and have thus reinforced the tendency to avoid contact. At other times, such as 1917–30, 1946–55, and 1963–66, Western hostility to the Soviet Union weakened the impulse of reformist Argentine governments to seek closer ties. In periods such as 1941–45, with the Grand Alliance, or in the détente era of the 1970s, Argentina had the opportunity to increase its contacts with the USSR without offending Great Britain or the United States, although at times if found itself in the uncomfortable position of upholding an anti-Soviet policy that the great powers had abandoned while receiving no tangible benefit (for example, between 1941 and 1946 or during the later years of Onganía's presidency).

The military coup of 1976 thus seems to have broken the cyclical rapprochement/rejection pattern. The reasons for this break with historical regularity are diverse and require different levels of explanation. On the international level, the military government after 1976 was faced with two basic problems, one economic, one political. The loss of Western European markets led to a search for new customers and ultimately to increased trade with the Soviet Union. In the international political arena, the military government's confrontation with the Western countries over Argentine human rights violations set the stage for rapprochement with a Soviet Union that displayed its pragmatism by protecting Argentina in international forums.

At the domestic political level, the Argentine military continued professing an extreme anticommunist ideology, but it altered the ranking of groups considered its most dangerous enemies. The pro-Soviet PCA was no longer regarded as an adversary worth eliminating, and the

USSR was no longer conceived of as a nation promoting class struggle. The main enemy was the guerrillas and their sources of support, who, although they classified themselves as Marxists, clearly neither took their orders from Moscow (whose actions they frequently denounced) nor had any direct relationship with the international, pro-Soviet communist movement. Obviously, this change of attitude did not mean the USSR and the PCA now had the ideological sympathy of the armed forces, but it did mean that both had come to enjoy a certain respectability, and the PCA was not exposed to the armed repression aimed at guerrilla groups of Peronist and Trotskyist leanings.

Finally, although important political changes might occur in Argentina, they will not lead to a deterioration in relations with the Soviet Union. Economic factors favoring ties will continue under any circumstances, and an elected government or a drastic alteration in the composition of the military regime could place in power groups less ideologically distant from the USSR. But whether or not an ideological or political shift of this magnitude occurs, the recurring cycle of rapprochement and rejection seems to have come to a definite end. Although the volume of trade might fluctuate, it is very unlikely the USSR would provoke any serious incidents, and any future government is unlikely to break or freeze relations on purely ideological grounds.

• Diplomacy and Strategy

Diplomatic relations between Argentina and the Soviet Union, established in 1946, were without importance until the beginning of the 1970s. True, in the first twenty-four years, Peronist and Radical governments (Perón, Frondizi, and Illia) did seek, for political reasons, closer relations with the USSR. But their declared intentions of balancing diplomatic ties with the West with better relations with the Soviet Union as a way of gaining greater autonomy in the international arena were usually no more than a mere expression of intent. Reluctantly, and attempting to incur a minimum of formal obligations, populist and reformist governments allowed themselves to be integrated into the hemispheric strategy of the United States. Argentina thus signed the Rio Treaty, joined the OAS, supported the Korean War and the expulsion of

Cuba from the OAS, and weakly protested U.S. intervention in the Dominican Republic. Their foreign policies offered only an appearance of independence and consisted of statements and speeches castigating the "two imperialisms" and placing objections to, and delaying as long as possible ratification of, regional agreements.

It was only after the Peronist return to power in 1973 that relations with the socialist bloc were strengthened and foreign policy became truly independent. But not even then did plans for closer diplomatic relations with the USSR fully succeed.

All previous experience would have predicted the opposite, but it was the 1976 military coup that produced the most far-reaching diplomatic rapprochement between the two countries. The USSR defended Argentina in international organizations over its human rights record and refrained from ideological and political attacks on the military government. Argentina abandoned all rhetorical and concrete confrontation with the Soviet Union and refused to join the grain embargo organized by the United States.

Beyond the factors already discussed, there are additional reasons of a political and diplomatic character that have contributed to the development of events. In addition to its basic economic interest, the Soviet Union seeks to use Argentina's singular position in South America to keep open one of its channels of communication in the region. In recent years, Soviet relations with Latin America in general have not been the most promising for a superpower wishing to maintain a worldwide presence. Relations with some governments have always been or have recently come to be chilly, unimportant, or even nonexistent. Argentina thus represents one of the few possibilities for maintaining some presence in the area, especially given the lack of Brazilian interest in Soviet approaches and the setbacks suffered in the military coup in Chile and the change of government in Peru. Despite its economic deterioration, Argentina continues to be one of the most important Latin American countries, and the ever present possibility of a resurgence of nationalist populism or reformism could lead to a confrontation with the United States and closer ties with the Soviet Union.

Soviet diplomatic support for Argentina is also related to the latter's continued participation in the nonaligned movement, even after the

military coup, and its relations with Cuba, especially economic links
that relieve the USSR of some of the burden of supporting the Cuban
economy in the face of the boycott imposed on it by most of the
hemisphere.

Finally, Argentina's friendly attitude at the time of the grain embargo
confirmed the Soviets in their belief that at some moment their investment of diplomatic good will would reap concrete benefits—economic,
political, and diplomatic.

From the Argentine government's perspective, diplomatic rapproachement with the USSR offers some undeniable advantages. Isolated within the Western world for its human rights violations, refusal to
ratify the nuclear nonproliferation treaty, and its border dispute with
Chile, Argentina has been grateful for all international diplomatic support, even from a country with which it has deep ideological differences. Argentine gratitude is reinforced by the Soviet Union's utter
lack of demands outside the economic sphere.

Common interests in the diplomatic sphere are beginning to expand
into military relations and nuclear cooperation. Thus far, military contacts have had few concrete results, although it is possible that the
Malvinas crisis and continuation of the border dispute with Chile could
lead to new developments. The Soviets seem to take greater interest in
expanding military contacts, especially with regard to arms sales which
would ease their trade deficit and establish firmer links requiring Argentine collaboration. The Argentine government, however, has been re-
luctant to purchase arms, probably because of the political and technical
difficulties involved, and seems likely to continue purchasing arms
from traditional Western suppliers despite recent difficulties.

In the nuclear field, the situation is the reverse, with Argentina more
interested in Soviet collaboration in order to obtain the materials required to continue its nuclear program. The Soviet Union, however,
does not seem very enthusiastic about supplying Argentina with nuclear material or technology, and sales were probably made only to
avoid offending the Argentine government. Another probable consid-
eration was the likelihood that the Argentine nuclear program is so
advanced that such materials could be produced in Argentina in the near
future anyway.

Argentine-Soviet diplomatic relations thus seem to have a solid foundation and are unlikely to be disrupted by the present or any future government. The military regime is unlikely to find similar support from another nation or group of nations of similar importance. Even if the military government is replaced by a constitutional regime, Soviet flexibility will adapt to the new circumstances, offering the new government equally beneficial relations.

• The Role of the PCA

The PCA's close relationship with the USSR merits analysis because of the role it plays and could play in the context of Argentine-Soviet relations. Obviously, the party constitutes a pressure group in favor of continuing and expanding bilateral ties, but it is necessary to evaluate the real importance of its presence in the development of contacts with the USSR.

In fact, the party's role in the development of such relations has been minimal. Its leaders and members seem to have had no direct influence on the initiation and evolution of relations, much less on any crucial decisions made by either government. The present state of the relationship is based on economic, political, and diplomatic circumstances on which party influence has been practically nil. "Reasons of state" have motivated the governments of both countries to seek closer ties, and not the pressure of a party that is virtually irrelevant in Argentine society, politics, and government.

If Argentine and Soviet leaders had not seen advantages in trade and diplomatic cooperation, no amount of propaganda on the part of the PCA could have led to the developments of the past few years. This is due both to the party's weakness in the Argentine political arena and to the fact that the Soviet Union does not base its international political and economic decisions on the interests and needs of such an unimportant ally as the PCA.

However, once closer ties began to develop, the PCA came to play a marginal but enthusiastic role in favor of improved Soviet-Argentine relations. Even though the party does not have the political weight to determine the course of events, it does have a solid organization and a certain propaganda capacity to be put at the service of those favoring expanded relations. Although its moderate support for the government—or for certain of its members—has caused discontent among PCA membership and has made it difficult to recruit new members, it has continued its support, and would probably only return to the opposition if relations with the USSR broke down or deteriorated. On the other hand, Argentine governments will probably continue to practice tolerance toward the PCA and its pro-Soviet propaganda activities so as not to introduce unnecessary tension into relations with the Soviets.

The PCA has made itself useful to the USSR by serving as a source of information on and interpreter of the Argentine political situation. Its activity seems to have consisted of supplying data and analysis on Argentine developments which the Soviets later bill as their own, which explains the total homogeneity of Soviet and PCA analyses in recent years. This type of assistance has helped the Soviet Union to defend a regime on the opposite extreme of the political spectrum, exposing it to international criticism which it has not been able to refute satisfactorily.

In the future, it seems unlikely that the PCA will come to play a major role in Argentine politics, although it will continue to be of minor use to both parties. At the same time, its defense of an unpopular military government seems likely to reduce its already minor role. Only a sharp sense of tactics and strategy—a sense the party has never displayed in the past—would allow it to be even a minor protagonist in political life as the country proceeds toward democratization. Otherwise, the party will continue without great success in its role as a pro-Soviet propagandist little listened to by the population and as a promoter of failed political alliances and institutional solutions.

• The Social Impact

Relations with the Soviet Union, especially economic ties, have had important repercussions on Argentine society. The most important development has been the emergence of powerful socioeconomic groups in favor of maintaining and expanding relations, a sentiment which hardly existed at the beginning of the 1970s.

Those groups directly benefiting from relations are in favor of their consolidation and are little disposed to abandon them for political or ideological reasons without finding a suitable replacement. Producers and exporters of meat and grain probably comprise the most powerful sector in the Argentine economy, and their decisions and interests have done much to shape modern Argentina. Although they lost some of their preeminence with the emergence of middle-class and populist parties, they continued to pressure or destabilize civilian governments and to direct the political and economic policies of military regimes.

For political, ideological, and social reasons, these sectors are suspicious of the Soviet Union and the PCA—fearing, with justification, that a leftward drift in Argentine politics would be harmful to their interests by resulting in measures such as the nationalization of foreign trade, expropriation of uncultivated land, agrarian reform, strict control of profits, and higher taxes, all of which are advocated by the Soviets and Argentine communists. But when the decision is between holding onto one's most important customer or giving into anticommunist fears, the former will always be preferred, as long as no equivalent markets are available and the communist threat is confined to the distant future.

The PCA would be threatened only if enactment of left-wing policies appeared imminent; the PCA has often been used as a scapegoat and the target of propaganda campaigns. Its selection as a scapegoat might be even more likely in an attempt to avoid damaging economic ties with the Soviet Union by attacking it directly. On the other hand, attempts by the Soviets to win diplomatic or political concessions would probably be initially resisted, then partially or totally granted, since Argentina's economic and even political survival depends on continued purchases by the USSR.

The maintenance of economic ties is less important for the Argentine industrial sector and state-owned enterprises, except for those that have already acquired equipment or are involved in joint enterprises with the Soviets. However, since the entire Argentine economy depends on the foreign currency earned by the agricultural sector, it is highly unlikely that these groups—or any other economic sector—would desire a reduction in trade with the USSR.

Of course, those sectors benefiting only indirectly from trade with the Soviets do not give it the same importance as those that do, and they are thus less susceptible to Soviet pressures outside the strictly economic sphere. But on the other hand, they tend to be less fiercely anticommunist than the agribusiness oligarchy and thus less fearful of closer diplomatic and political ties with the USSR that would permit Argentina to pursue an independent and nonaligned foreign policy.

Thus, a stable configuration of socioeconomic interest in favor of closer ties with the Soviet Union has emerged. The agricultural interests are concerned to restrict relations inasmuch as possible to the strictly economic sphere, but a certain opening exists to Soviet diplomatic and political advances, provided they do not suggest an explicit and formal alliance. The USSR seems likely to continue its extremely pragmatic policy toward Argentina, making gradual progress toward its diplomatic and strategic goals, but without making any moves that could be interpreted as open pressure.

• The Malvinas Crisis and After

Tensions in relations with the United States, Canada, and the Western European nations produced by the Malvinas crisis have served to increase the Argentine tendency toward closer ties with the Soviet Union.

The decision to take possession of the islands, which had been occupied by Britain since 1833 and whose status had been the subject of negotiation for many years, seems to have been taken without any adequate analysis of the consequences. The military government supposed that the United States, grateful for Argentine cooperation in Central America and a generally pro-American foreign policy, would assume a position of benevolent neutrality and act discreetly to restrain the British response. The government also seems to have counted on European apathy, unconditional and tangible support from the rest of Latin America and the Third World, and a weak response from Britain restricted to diplomatic protests. The USSR and the socialist bloc were apparently of no importance in the government's strategy, except perhaps to offer verbal support as a reflection of traditional hostility toward Great Britain.

The Argentine government was faced with a desperate situation when the United States sided openly with Britain, offering both diplomatic and military support; the EEC countries adopted economic sanctions; Latin American and Third World support proved to be strictly rhetorical; and Britain launched a large military expedition to recover the islands. The Soviet Union abstained from voting on a British resolution submitted to the UN Security Council condemning Argentina, and made known its support for Argentina. Obviously the Soviet position eased the way for further rapprochement between the two countries. Argentina needed international allies who could help stop the British advance, while the Soviets were motivated by economic interests, hostility to Britain and the United States, and the chance to exploit tensions within the Western Hemisphere. The disastrous end to the crisis convinced the military government of the need for powerful and relatively reliable allies, and none was available apart from the USSR.

The Argentine military is also interested in quickly replacing the huge losses of equipment suffered in the conflict. It thus might be willing to make arms purchases from the Soviet Union if Western countries continue to refuse to sell sophisticated weaponry to Argentina. The Soviets, for their part, are eager to make arms sales, both to ease their chronic trade deficit with Argentina and to create new ties that will strengthen Argentine interest in continued relations.

The resentment felt by the majority of the Argentine population against the role played by the United States and Western Europe in the conflict—reflected in huge demonstrations, in the mass media, and in the declarations of the formerly pro-Western military government—has added a new element favoring closer ties with the Soviets. These anti-Western sentiments are likely to remain strong for some time to come, and will affect the foreign policy of all governments in the foreseeable future. In general, public opinion in Argentina feels betrayed by the West and considers the Rio Treaty an instrument at the service of only one of its members—the United States. In contrast, the Soviets, despite ideological and political differences, are regarded as a nation worthy of friendship and respect, even though it is acknowledged that they are pursuing their own interests and goals.

None of the above suggests, however, that Argentina is going to become an open ally of the Soviet Union, much less be drawn into the

Soviet sphere of influence or serve as a Soviet beachhead in South America. Too many factors work against such a development, including the fierce anticommunism of the military and conservative civilian sectors; skepticism about Soviet motives among the populist, center-left, and even left-wing parties; lack of cultural and ideological affinity; and the fear of adverse reactions from both the Western countries and domestic opponents of political rapproachement. Neither is it clear that the USSR wants an open alliance, which might aggravate international tensions and require new economic and military commitments far from its borders.

If international tensions do increase, Argentina seems likely to adopt a position of benevolent neutrality toward the USSR, similar to its policy toward fascist regimes before and during most of World War II. The principal difference is that the earlier policy was based on political and ideological sympathies, while economic interests are paramount in the Soviet relationship.

If the Western countries attempt to reverse the course of Argentine-Soviet relations, they will meet with considerable obstacles, both political and economic. Given the power of producers, traders, and exporters in the United States and the EEC, they are unlikely to be able to offer Argentina similar guarantees to the Soviets in the volume and pricing of exports. And any political or diplomatic advantages offered Argentina would have to be considerable to overcome the hostility generated by the Malvinas crisis.

In conclusion, the web of shared interests appears to be solid and destined to expand. The discreet partnership between Argentina and the Soviet Union has ceased to be a matter of temporary convenience and has become a constant in international relations for the foreseeable future.

Notes

Bibliography

Index

Notes

• *Chapter 1. Intermittent Ties: Argentina and the Soviet Union,*
1917–1970

1. For a discussion of the privileged status of the Argentine legation, see Cheston,
Diplomatic Sideshow, pp. 159–60.

2. Ibid., p. 160; Clissold, *Soviet Relations*, p. 8.

3. Cheston, *Diplomatic Sideshow*, p. 159. Only in 1931 did Stein leave his diplomatic
post to take up residence in the United States.

4. Telegram to the Argentinian minister, Dok. Vnesh. Pol. VI (1962), no. 137,
pp. 240–41, reproduced in Clissold, *Soviet Relations*, p. 159.

5. Cf. Cheston, *Diplomatic Sideshow*, pp. 163–65.

6. For an interesting and detailed analysis of Kraevsky's personality and early activities in the United States and South America, see ibid., pp. 167–74.

7. Ibid., pp. 175–76.

8. Ibid., pp. 176–77; Clissold, *Soviet Relations*, p. 118.

9. Cheston, *Diplomatic Sideshow*, p. 184; Muñiz Ortega, *La URSS y América Latina*,
p. 22.

10. Frondizi, *Petróleo y política*, pp. 249–59.

11. See Muñiz Ortega, *La URSS y América Latina*, p. 22, taken from the *Economic
Political Guide* (Moscow, 1962), p. 110.

12. For an account of Yrigoyen's anticolonialist views and his plans to develop an
independent foreign policy, see Luna, *Yrigoyen*, pp. 225–39.

13. Cf. Cheston, *Diplomatic Sideshow*, pp. 196–97.

14. Ibid., pp. 267–68.

15. The characteristics of the military coup of 1930 and the ideology and actions of the
provisional government are discussed in Schillizzi Moreno, *Argentina contemporánea*
1:15–136.

16. See Cheston, *Diplomatic Sideshow*, pp. 269–70, for an account of the presentation
of this proposal.

17. This interpretation can be found in a *Buenos Aires Herald* editorial of 12 August
1931, cited in Cheston, *Diplomatic Sideshow*, p. 270.

18. Frondizi offers this interpretation in *Petróleo y política*, pp. 252–59.

19. Clissold, *Soviet Relations*, pp. 8–9, 118; Muñiz Ortega, *La URSS y América
Latina*, p. 24.

20. For an account of the raid and its consequences, see Cheston, *Diplomatic Sideshow*, pp. 271–74.

21. Valtin, *Sans patrie ni frontière*, cited in Clissold, *Soviet Relations*, p. 62.

22. Cheston, *Diplomatic Sideshow*, pp. 175, 216, from U.S. National Archives, Department of State Document No. 835.00B/6, 24 August, 1927.

23. *Pravda*, 13, 17 August 1931, cited in Cheston, *Diplomatic Sideshow*, pp. 274–75. An interpretation that attributes the raid to the domestic political situation and international pressures was offered years later by the Argentine Senator Lisandro de la Torre in the course of a debate on the law against communism (see "Debate sobre el comunismo," Sesión de la Cámara de Senadores del 21 de diciembre de 1936, in Amaral, *Anecdotario de Lisandro de la Torre*, pp. 259–62).

24. Cheston, *Diplomatic Sideshow*, pp. 278–79.

25. For a discussion of Argentine dependency on Great Britain, see for example Irazusta, *Influencia económica británica;* and Scalabrini Ortiz, *Política británica*.

26. On the origin of the Partido Comunista Argentino and its evolution, see PCA, *Esbozo de historia del Partido Comunista;* Alexander, *Communism in Latin America*, pp. 154–56.

27. Cheston, *Diplomatic Sideshow*, pp 295–96.

28. League of Nations, Verbatim Record of the Fifteenth Ordinary Session of the League of Nations—Ninth Plenary Meeting (18 September 1934), cited in Cheston, *Diplomatic Sideshow*, pp. 160–61n.

29. League of Nations, Official Journal, Seventeenth Year, February 1936, cited in Clissold, *Soviet Relations*, p. 116.

30. League of Nations, Official Journal, Twentieth Year, November–December 1939, cited in Clissold, *Soviet Relations*, pp. 116–17.

31. Díaz Araujo provides a sympathetic account of the motivations, ideology, and objectives of the officers who took power in June 1943 in *La conspiración del 43*. For a different perspective, see Potash, *El ejército y la política en la Argentina, 1928–1943*.

32. See the article by F. Glibovsky in *Voina i Robochni clas*, no. 16, 15 August 1944, cited in Clissold, *Soviet Relations*, pp. 172–73.

33. Braden provides a personal account of his activities in Argentina during this period and of his relations with the military government, especially with Perón, in *Diplomats and Demagogues*, pp. 316–38.

34. An interesting description and analysis of the events relating to the diplomatic battle among the USSR, the United States, and the Latin American countries over Argentina's admission to the United Nations can be found in Green, *The Containment of Latin America*, pp. 165–67, 215–20, 237–54.

35. Excerpts from Molotov's speech at the San Francisco conference on 30 April 1945 are reprinted in Clissold, *Soviet Relations*, pp. 173–74.

36. See the article by L. Volinksy, "The role Argentina is playing," *New Times*, 1 June 1945, cited in Clissold, *Soviet Relations*, p. 174.

37. *Pravda*, 7 June 146, cited in Clissold, *Soviet Relations*, p. 174.

38. See the *Pravda* commentary of 9 June 1946, cited in Clissold, *Soviet Relations,* pp. 175–76.

39. See Bramuglia's declarations, cited in Muñiz Ortega, *La URSS y América Latina,* pp. 45–46.

40. Interview with Federico Cantoni in *Los Andes* (Mendoza, Argentina), cited in Muñiz Ortega, *La URSS y América Latina,* p. 46. Cantoni appointed Leopoldo Bravo as embassy secretary, a protégé of his in the Unión Cívica Radical Bloquista, a small political group limited to San Juan Province. Bravo later became ambassador in Moscow during 1953–55 and again after the 1976 military coup.

41. For a description of Peronist international policy, see Perón, *Doctrina peronista,* pp. 319–36.

42. Bagú, *Argentina en el mundo,* pp. 105–06; Green, *The Containment of Latin America,* pp. 276–83; Parkinson, *Latin America, the Cold War and the World Powers,* p. 15.

43. Green, *The Containment of Latin America,* pp. 276–83; Parkinson, *Latin America, the Cold War and the World Powers,* pp. 15–16.

44. Conil Paz and Ferrari, *Argentina's Foreign Policy,* p. 168.

45. Parkinson, *Latin America, the Cold War and the World Powers,* p. 20n.

46. See *Slavyane* (Moscow), November 1949, cited in Clissold, *Soviet Relations,* pp. 176–77, for the Soviet denunciation of the closing of the Slav Union, a PCA front group. At this time the Cominform had expelled Yugoslavia and was engaged in a propaganda campaign against Tito's "deviationism."

47. For a discussion of Perón's position with regard to the Korean crisis and the possibility of sending Argentine troops, see Potash, *The Army and Politics in Argentina,* pp. 120–21.

48. Parkinson discusses Perón's changes in position in *Latin America, the Cold War and the World Powers,* pp. 22–23.

49. References to the meeting appear in "Stalin and Bravo," *The World Today* 9, no. 2 (February 1953): 97–98.

50. Muñiz Ortega, *La URSS y América Latina,* pp. 62–63; Tomberg, *Relaciones económicas,* p. 53.

51. Estremadoyro, *Relaciones económicas de Argentina,* pp. 8–9.

52. Alexander, *Communism in Latin America,* pp. 171–75.

53. Muñiz Ortega, *La URSS y América Latina,* pp. 62–63; Tomberg, *Relaciones económicas,* p. 53.

54. Another factor in the PCA's support was Frondizi's principal adviser, Rogelio Frigerio, an industrialist with old contacts in leftist sectors who employed Marxist concepts to promote the development of a powerful national bourgeoisie, state ownership of strategic industries, and a class alliance. Frondizi's *Petróleo y política* also seemed to rely on Marxist methodology and, moreover, supported the expansion of economic relations with the USSR.

55. Clark, *Latin American Economic Relations,* p. 157; Muñiz Ortega, *La URSS y América Latina,* pp. 67–68.

56. Tomberg, *Relaciones económicas*, p. 54.

57. These military statements generally consisted of a series of political and economic demands presented to Frondizi by leading officers and had the character of ultimatums. In most cases Frondizi gave in, and bit by bit his image as a skilled political manipulator was eroded until he became a virtual prisoner of the armed forces. Having already lost the support of the Peronists, his own party was torn apart by internal conflicts. Almost one hundred statements were issued and resulted in, among other things, the removal of Frigerio, changes in economic policy, persecution of Peronism and communism, annulling of elections, and so forth.

58. Clissold, *Soviet Relations*, p. 33.

59. Ibid. The embassy staff was reduced to ten accredited diplomats and twenty-two nonaccredited staff.

60. See the article in *Izvestiya*, 6 June 1961, cited in Clissold, *Soviet Relations*, pp. 177–79.

61. For an account of this period, see Luna, *De Perón a Lanusse*, pp. 145–68.

62. Estremadoyro, *Relaciones económicas de Argentina*, p. 8; Tomberg, *Relaciones económicas*, p. 54.

63. For a discussion of UCRP ideology, see Vacs, *La Unión Cívica Radical*. The Illia government's domestic and foreign policies are discussed in several articles in Selser, *El Onganiato*.

64. *International Affairs*, no. 12 (December 1963), cited in Clissold, *Soviet Relations*, p. 179.

65. Tomberg, *Relaciones económicas*, p. 54.

66. See the "Estatuto y Actas Basicas de la 'Revolución Argentina' in Selser, *El Onganiato* 1:300–10.

67. For a discussion of the law of defense against communism, see Selser, *El Onganiato* 2:245–54, 261–73, 277–93.

68. The bases for this policy are revealed in works by some members of the Argentine military, including Marini, *Estrategia sin tiempo;* and Villegas, *Guerra revolucionaria comunista*. Both these works had great influence on the formulation of national security ideology and ideological frontiers prevalent in the armed forces.

69. For an account of the incident and the declaration of the foreign minister, Costa Méndez, see Selser, *El Onganiato* 2:238. Clissold, *Soviet Relations*, reprints the Soviet protest on pp. 179–80.

70. The Argentine government's note on the Soviet invasion of Czechoslovakia appears in Clissold, *Soviet Relations*, p. 180.

71. *New York Times*, 31 March 1970.

72. Ibid., 11 June 1970.

73. Although much of the population openly or tacitly supported the coup in 1966, the Onganía government quickly became unpopular. In 1969 accumulated popular discontent produced a series of labor and student uprisings that culminated in the *Cordobazo* of May 1969, an urban insurrection that severely weakened the government. Although Onganía held onto power for more than a year, increasing political, social, economic, and military tensions forced him to resign in June 1970.

• *Chapter 2. The Endless Spiral: Economic Ties Since 1970*

1. For a discussion of the so-called hegemonic stalemate in Argentina in the early 1970s, see Braun, *El capitalismo argentino en crisis.*

2. Excellent analyses of the Argentine situation during this period and of the interaction among economic, political, and social variables can be found in ibid; Portantiero, "Economía y política en la crisis argentina." For an insider's view written by one of the era's principal protagonists, see Lanusse, *Mi testimonio.*

3. Lanusse, *Mi testimonio,* pp. 240–43.

4. Républica Argentina, Ministerio de Economía, Hacienda y Finanzas, *Anuario estadístico 1980,* p. 523.

5. Tomberg, *Relaciones económicas,* p. 54.

6. The complete text of the agreement can be found in CEPAL (ECLA), *Recopilación de convenios, acuerdos y protocolos vigentes* 1:45–48.

7. CEPAL (ECLA), *Relaciones económicas entre América Latina y los paises miembros del CAME,* p. 17.

8. On the other hand, bilateral payment agreements were abandoned because of the difficulties they caused Argentina. The agreement signed in 1953 included this clause, but Argentina was unable to meet import quotas established for Soviet products, and the resulting favorable balances had to be liquidated under disadvantageous circumstances. See Clark, *Latin American Economic Relations,* pp. 250–53; Fichet, "Tres decenios de relaciones."

9. A review of this period can be found in Landi, "Argentina 1973–1976." The October 1973–March 1976 period is reviewed in the same article and in Landi, "La tercera presidencia de Perón."

10. Tuzmujavédov, "La no alineación: ¿etapa latinoamericana?" An interesting discussion of the interrelationships among economic dependence, domestic situations, and foreign policy in Latin American nations can be found in a series of articles by Soviet specialists published under the title "América Latina: Política exterior y dependencia económica."

11. For a discussion of the Gelbard team's economic strategy, see the two Landi articles cited in note 9 and Wynia, *Argentina in the Postwar Era,* pp. 203–24.

12. In Argentina, nontraditional exports are generally considered to be everything but meat, grain, hides, wool, and similar primary products.

13. For an account of the Gelbard visit to Cuba, see Fidel Castro, "Misión Gelbard: el fin del cerco."

14. *New York Times,* 7 August 1973; *Wall Street Journal,* 7 August 1973; *Journal of Commerce,* 30 August 1973. For an account of Argentine trade with Cuba during this period, see Estremadoyro, *Relaciones económicas de Argentina,* pp. 66–76.

15. *Clarín,* 8 December 1976. According to available information, at that time similar joint chambers of commerce existed only in the following countries: France, Italy, Japan, Belgium/Luxemburg, and the United States. There was also an Arab-Soviet chamber of commerce.

16. See CEPAL (ECLA), *Recopilación de convenios*, pp. 48–50.

17. The agreement was ratified by Argentina in 1977. The delay was linked to changes in the Argentine political scene between 1974 and 1976.

18. Estremadoyro, *Relaciones económicas de Argentina*, p. 17; Tomberg, *Relaciones económicas*, pp. 54–55.

19. This agreement was ratified only in 1977, but it had been in provisional force since its signing.

20. Tomberg, *Relaciones económicas*, p. 55. This agreement too was only ratified in 1977.

21. See Estremadoyro, *Relaciones económicas de Argentina*, pp. 59-62. For a description of the dam and hydroelectric plant at Salto Grande, see *Economic Information on Argentina*.

22. *New York Times*, 7, 8 May 1974.

23. *Miami Herald*, 21 May 1974.

24. *New York Times*, 8 May 1974. On 27 May 1974 the Argentine economics ministry announced that reports on the granting of a loan were inaccurate (Argentine sources had leaked the information in Moscow on 7 May), and final figures were not yet available (*Washington Post*, 9 June 1974).

25. Tomberg, *Relaciones económicas*, p. 61.

26. Ibid., p. 57.

27. CEPAL (ECLA), *Informe de la Secretaría*, p. 20.

28. Ibid., pp. 20–22.

29. Estremadoyro, *Relaciones económicas de Argentina*, pp. 61–62.

30. Ibid., p. 61.

31. Ibid., pp. 59, 63; Tomberg, *Relaciones económicas*, p. 56.

32. *Christian Science Monitor*, 8 July 1974.

33. Ratification of this agreement was also delayed until 1977.

34. Tomberg, *Relaciones económicas*, p. 56.

35. Ibid., pp. 56–57.

36. *Journal of Commerce*, 24 September 1974.

37. Ibid., 16 October 1974.

38. Ibid., 17 October 1974.

39. For accounts of the situation produced by the death of Perón, see Landi, "Argentina 1973–1976," and "La tercera presidencia de Perón"; Wynia, *Argentina in the Postwar Era*, pp. 222–27.

40. Landi, "La tercera presidencia de Perón," p. 1938. The magazine *Cabildo*, belonging to a nationalist, ultrarightist group with fascist, antiliberal, anticommunist, and anti-Semitic leanings (Gelbard was Jewish), featured prominently in this campaign. Despite its small circulation, its views found favor among certain sectors of the armed forces, and even in the government. But liberal-conservative sectors, right-wing Peronists, and certain leftist groups also joined in the campaign against Gelbard's domestic and foreign economic policies.

41. Tomberg, *Relaciones económicas*, pp. 56–57.

42. According to Argentine sources, the country's total installed capacity in 1979 was

9.57 million kilowatts; this included hydroelectric, thermoelectric, and nuclear power plants. See República Argentina, *Anuario estadístico*, p. 394.

43. The Middle Paraná project and the contract with the Soviets are discussed in Tomberg, *Relaciones económicas*, pp. 61–62; *El Economista*, 27 June 1975.

44. *Journal of Commerce*, 29 September 1975.

45. Terekhov, "Soviet-Argentine Trade Relations"; Tomberg, *Relaciones económicas*, pp. 59, 63.

46. The majority of agreements signed with the USSR contain clauses establishing that part of the products used to repay credits must be manufactured or semimanufactured.

47. Martínez de Hoz's economic program and its evolution over time are discussed in Républica Argentina, Ministerio de Economía, *Memoria (29-3-1976/29-3-1981)*.

48. Analysis of Martínez de Hoz's policy and its results can be found in Canitrot, *La disciplina como objetivo;* and "Teoría y práctica del liberalismo."

49. Tomberg, *Relaciones económicas*, p. 58.

50. *Novedades de la Unión Soviética* (Buenos Aires), 15 October 1976; *Clarín*, 8 November 1976.

51. *New York Times*, 4, 5 November 1976; *Washington Post*, 5 November 1976.

52. Ministerio de Agricultura y Ganadería, Junta Nacional de Granos, *Anuario 1981*, pp. 2, 5, 7, 10, 13; Onis, "Record Argentine grain harvest"; Bono, "Argentina makes agressive comeback."

53. Ministerio de Agricultura y Ganadería, Junta Nacional de Granos, *Anuario 1981*, pp. 63, 69, 74, 79.

54. For an example of the manipulations practiced by Bunge and Born—a multinational of Argentine origin presently headquartered in Curacao for tax purposes—see Robbins, "Inquiry widening on grain exports"; "Bunge is a worldwide concern that is shrouded in mystery." An interesting analysis of the history and activities of the leading international grain-trading companies can be found in Morgan, *Merchants of Grain*.

55. Secretaría de Agricultura y Ganadería, Junta Nacional de Carnes, *Síntesis estadística: Año 1979*, p. 152.

56. Tomberg, *Relaciones económicas*, p. 88.

57. Estremadoyro, *Relaciones económicas de Argentina*, p. 65.

58. *New York Times*, 2, 3 October 1977.

59. Ibid., 9 October 1977; *América Latina*, no. 2 (1978): 16–17.

60. According to calculations based on data released by the Ministerio de Agricultura y Ganadería, Junta Nacional de Granos, *Anuario 1981*.

61. *La Opinión*, 10 November 1978; *La Nación*, 2 July 1978.

62. *La Prensa*, 3 December 1981.

63. *Mercado*, 28 July 1979.

64. According to data published by the Junta Nacional de Granos and compared with those provided by the Secretaría de Comercio in the *Boletín Semanal de Economía*, no. 439, 3 May 1982.

65. Estimates based on data provided by the Secretaría de Agricultura y Ganadería, Junta Nacional de Carnes, *Síntesis Estadística*.

66. *Washington Post*, 8 January 1980.

67. Ibid., 11 January 1980.

68. *Financial Times*, 15 January 1980.

69. *Confirmado* (Bunenos Aires), 24 January 1980.

70. *Washington Post*, 25 January 1980; *Christian Science Monitor*, 28 January 1980.

71. *Washington Post*, 25 January 1980; *Financial Times*, 31 January 1980.

72. *Los Angeles Times*, 31 January 1980; *New York Times*, 1 February 1980.

73. Secretaría de Agricultura y Gandería, Junta Nacional de Granos, *Anuario 1981*.

74. *Los Angeles Times*, 27 February 1980; *Journal of Commerce*, 3 March 1980; *New York Times*, 26 March 1980.

75. *Los Andes*, 21 May 1981.

76. *Somos* (Argentina), 1 May 1981.

77. See also the declarations on this subject of the subsecretary for international negotiations and organizations, Alfredo Espósito, in *Clarín*, 17 May 1981.

78. *Journal of Commerce*, 17 April 1980.

79. República Argentina, Ministerio de Economía, *Boletín Semanal de Economía*, no. 423 (4 January 1982).

80. *Wall Street Journal*, 14 July 1980; *New York Times*, 17 July 1980; *Latin American Commodities Report*, 18 July 1980; *La Nación*, 24 July 1980.

81. Zinovyev, "Soviet economic links with Latin America."

82. *Washington Post*, 13 January 1981; *Financial Times*, 17 March 1981.

83. Cf. *Latin American Commodities Report*, 22 May 1981.

84. *Clarín*, 23, 24, 25 April 1981.

85. Calculated on the basis of data released by the Junta Nacional de Granos in March 1982.

86. *Clarín*, 10 May 1982.

87. For accounts of the visit of the Soviet trade mission and its results, see *Clarín*, 16, 19, 20 May 1981; *Los Andes*, 6, 12, 16, 17, 19 May 1981; *La Nación*, 17 May 1981.

88. For accounts of the visit of the Argentine trade mission to Moscow, see *Clarín*, 16 and 23 June 1981; *Los Andes*, 4, 13, and 16 June 1981; *La Prensa*, 21 June 1981.

89. *Clarín*, 23 June 1981.

90. República Argentina, Ministerio de Economía, *Boletín Semanal de Economía*, no. 439, (3 May 1982).

91. For a description of the Yaciretá dam and some of the problems with the bidding system, see *Convicción*, 12 August 1981. On the awarding of contracts, see *La Prensa*, 12 September 1981.

92. *La Prensa*, 16, 17 September 1981.

93. *La Opinión*, 20 March 1981.

94. *La Prensa*, 21 March 1981.

95. For a report on the fourth meeting of the Argentine-Soviet joint commission, see República Argentina, Ministerio de Economía, *Boletín Semanal de Economía*, nos. 437, 438 (19, 26 April 1982).

96. For other statistics on foreign trade with selected countries and areas, see República Argentina, *Anuario Estadístico*, pp. 523–25.

97. For the composition of Argentina exports for the 1966–79 period, see ibid., pp. 521–22.

98. For a discussion of the military government's economic policy in this respect, see Canitrot, *La disciplina como objetivo*, and "Teoría y práctica del liberalismo."

99. Cf. the projections made by the Junta Nacional de Granos in República Argentina, Ministerio de Economía, *Boletín Semanal de Economía*, no 436 (5 April 1982).

100. *Somos*, no. 241 (1 May 1981).

101. *Clarín*, 23 April 1981.

102. *Ultima Clave*, no. 474 (15 April 1980).

103. *La Nación*, 23 May 1981.

104. *Buenos Aires Herald*, 21 May 1981.

105. Declarations by Bameule in *Somos*, no. 241 (1 May 1981).

106. *La Nación*, 24 April 1981.

107. *La Prensa*, 26 June 1980.

108. República Argentina, Ministerio de Economía, Hacienda y Finanzas, *Información Económica de la Argentina*, no. 119 (July–August 1981).

109. *La Prensa*, 26 June 1980; *Convicción*, 25 June 1980; *El Día*, 22 February 1980; *Newsweek*, 4 August 1980.

110. *Clarín*, 6 August 1980.

111. Ibid., 29 May 1981; *Washington Post*, 7 May 1981; *Latin American Commodities Report*, 28 August 1981.

• *Chapter 3. Converging Interests: Diplomacy and Military Contacts*

1. In Argentina, Brazil has long been considered a rival for South American leadership. Military governments in particular view Brazil as a dangerous neighbor with expansionist aims. See Scenna, *Argentina-Brasil: Cuatro siglos de rivalidad*.

2. The 1971 commercial agreement is discussed in chapter 2.

3. These pressures and the role played by the military in the Argentine political scene are described in Potash, *The Army and Politics in Argentina;* and Rouquié, *Pouvoir militaire et société politique*.

4. A few, by no means exhaustive, examples: Martínez de Hoz was minister of economics after the coup that deposed Frondizi and again after 1976; Nicanor Costa Méndez was foreign minister under Onganía and again under Galtieri; and Amadeo Frugoli, defense minister in 1982, had already headed the ministry of social welfare under Levingston.

5. Cámpora, *La revolución peronista*, p. 12. This is a collection of speeches made by the candidate and later president during his electoral campaign and first days in office.

6. *La Prensa*, 26 May 1973.

7. See Cámpora, *La revolución peronista*, pp. 96–107.

8. Sobel, *Argentina and Perón*, p. 86.

9. *New York Times*, 7 August 1973; *Journal of Commerce*, 8, 30 August 1973.

10. *Washington Post*, 11 August 1973.

11. For a moderate Peronist politician's view of this problem, see Luder, *Argentina en Latinoamerica*. Luder was provisional president of the Senate in 1975–76 and provisional president of the republic for a brief period in 1975. Leftist Peronist publications, including *Militancia* and *El descamisado*, regarded the problem as fundamental, as did the non-Peronist left in general.

12. Attacks on the Pinochet regime in the Soviet press have been too numerous to cite individually. Titles of a few representative articles published in 1974 reflect the general tone: "The butchers of Chile must be brought to book!" *New Times*, no. 13 (April 1974): 1; "Gorillas in judge's togas," ibid., no. 20 (May 1974): 7; "End the terror," ibid., no. 26 (June 1974): 8; "Stop the political terror in Chile," ibid., no. 33 (August 1974): 30–31. On Uruguay: "Why Arismendi is persecuted," ibid., no. 21 (May 1974): 6; "Uruguay: 3 years of dictatorship," ibid., no. 28 (July 1976): 12; "Mounting resistance," ibid., no. 21 (May 1977): 12. Similar denunciations can be found throughout the whole of the 1973–82 period in publications such as *World Marxist Review, World Marxist Review Information Bulletin, América Latina,* and *International Affairs*, all published in the USSR.

13. In contrast to the attacks on Chile and Uruguay, the author has been unable to locate even one article criticizing the Argentine military dictatorship in similar terms.

14. Kosichev, "Argentina: troubled times," *New Times*, no. 43 (October 1974): 10–11.

15. See chapter 2 for a discussion of the Soviet trade mission visit and Gelbard's visit to Moscow.

16. *New York Times*, 7, 8, 12 May 1974; Orlov, "Soviet-Argentine relations: New stage."

17. Kosichev, "Argentina: troubled times"; Orlov, "Soviet-Argentine relations: New stage"; Seryogin, "Argentina: confrontation of the forces of democracy and reaction."

18. For accounts of the political, economic, and social crisis under Isabel Perón's government, see Landi, "Argentina 1973–1976," and "La tercera presidencia de Perón"; Wynia, *Argentina in the Postwar Era*, pp. 222–27. On the last months of the Peronist government, see the account by one of the defense ministers during this period, Deheza, *Marzo 23, hora 24*.

19. Seryogin, "Argentina: confrontation of the forces of democracy and reaction."

20. Chirkov, "Coup that was expected."

21. *La Prensa*, 25 May 1976.

22. Ibid.

23. Ibid., 25, 26, 27 May 1976.

24. TELAM, 3, 6 April 1976.

25. *Miami Herald*, 5 April 1976.

26. Maksinenko, "Coup d'etat in Argentina"; Karmen, "Military junta in power."

27. TASS, 27 March 1976.

28. Lozza, "Whither Argentina?"

29. *New York Times*, 4, 5 November 1976. For the impressions of one of these technicians on Argentina, in an article combining local color with political observations but curiously ignoring the incident, see Simorra, "Argentine tango."

30. On the human rights situation in Argentina, see Organization of American States, Interamerican Commission on Human Rights, *Report on the Situation of Human Rights in Argentina,* which covers the years 1976 to 1979.

31. Stoetzer, *Two Studies,* p. 79.

32. Ibid., p. 78.

33. *Latin American Political Report* 11, no. 7 (18 February 1977): 51.

34. Ibid., 11, no. 34 (2 September 1977): 267–68; *Washington Post,* 11 November 1977.

35. Baryshev, "In search of a way out."

36. *Los Angeles Times,* 2, 3 October 1977; *New York Times,* 2, 3 October 1977; TELAM, 1, 2 October 1977.

37. *La Prensa,* 4 October 1977.

38. *Izvestiya,* 7 October 1977.

39. *TELAM,* 3 October 1977.

40. *TELAM,* 4 October 1977; *Latin American Political Report* 11, no. 40 (14 October 1977): 314.

41. *TELAM,* 6 October 1977.

42. *Convicción,* 25 January 1981. These remarks constituted a review of his ambassadorship in Moscow, made by Bravo shortly before returning to Argentina to assume the governorship of San Juan Province.

43. Smirnov, "Who's stirring up trouble at Cape Horn?"

44. Ibid.

45. David Belnap, "Argentina warms up to Soviet ties."

46. Ibid.

47. *Latin American Political Report,* 13, no. 36 (14 September 1979): 284.

48. Baryshev, "Argentina: Pressing problems."

49. *La Prensa,* 11 January 1980.

50. Ibid.

51. *Financial Times,* 15 January 1980.

52. *La Prensa,* 18 January 1980.

53. *Washington Post,* 25 January 1980; *Los Angeles Times,* 27 January 1980; *Ultima Clave,* 29 January 1980.

54. *Clarín,* 25 January 1980.

55. *Ultima Clave,* 15 April 1980.

56. *Clarín,* 30 January 1980; *Los Angeles Times,* 31 January 1980.

57. *Clarín,* 17 May 1980.

58. *Convicción,* 30 July 1980.

59. *New Times,* no. 14 (April 1980): 11.

60. Ibid., no. 19 (May 1981): 27.

61. *La Nación,* 8 July 1981; *El Mercurio,* 27 June 1981.

62. *Miami Herald,* 24 July 1981; *Washington Post,* 26 July 1981; *New York Times,* 27 July 1981.

63. For Argentine press treatment of proposed Argentine participation in the Sinai

peacekeeping force and the Soviet warning against it, see *La Nación*, 2 August 1981; *La Prensa*, 8 August 1981.

64. *La Prensa*, 2 October 1981.

65. Ibid., 12 December 1981; *Noticias Argentinas*, 24 December 1981.

66. *Izvestiya*, 13 January 1982; *La Prensa*, 12 January 1982.

67. *TELAM*, 30 December 1981; *Newsweek*, 18 January 1982, p. 23.

68. *La Prensa*, 12, 23 January 1982.

69. *Noticias Argentinas*, 24 February 1982.

70. *La Nación*, 3 February 1982.

71. *Noticias Argentinas*, 5 February 1982.

72. Ibid., 12 February 1982.

73. *La Prensa*, 5 March 1982.

74. The events of 2 April 1982 and subsequent developments were given full coverage in both the U.S. and Argentine press, including *La Prensa, Clarín, La Nación,* the *Washington Post,* and the *New York Times.*

75. Vyacheslav Rostovtsev, speaking on the Moscow radio program, "Talking to You," 11 May 1982.

76. Soviet analyses of the Anglo-Argentine conflict reflecting this interpretation were numerous; see *Pravda, Izvestiya, Novoye Vremya,* etc.

77. Another interesting, although secondary, factor favoring closer ties was the sympathy the Soviet Union seemed to enjoy among the Argentine population (in contrast to the hostility felt toward Great Britain, the United States, and most Western European nations, with the exceptions of Ireland and Italy). A dramatic example of this new attitude was the rousing ovations given a Soviet soccer team in Buenos Aires in April 1982. (See *La Prensa,* 16 April 1982.)

78. *Krasnaia Zvezda*, 29 November 1975.

79. See *La Prensa*, 19, 20, 21, 22, 23 December 1975, for accounts of the failed air force coup.

80. Regarding the exchange of visits by Argentine and Soviet military missions, see *Buenos Aires Herald,* 23 August 1979; *Ultima Clave,* 28 August 1979; *Miami Herald,* 23 August 1979; *Los Angeles Times,* 25 August 1979, 27 February 1980.

81. *New York Times,* 9 September 1979; *Latin American Political Report* 13, no. 37 (21 September 1979): 293–94.

82. *Washington Post,* 13 January 1981; *Financial Times,* 17 March 1981.

83. *La Prensa,* 21 March 1982.

• Chapter 4. Manifest Consequences: Political and Social Effects

1. Central Committee of the CPA, "The dictatorship's 'political plan' and the communist position," pp. 24–25.

2. Ibid., p. 26.

3. Ibid., p. 29.

4. See CPA, "For a democratic national life," pp. 66–69; Central Committee of the CPA, "Unity and struggle," pp. 40–49.

5. "Los comunistas y la institucionalización del país," report presented to the executive committee of the PCA (29–30 April 1972), in Arnedo Alvarez, *Cuatro décadas,* pp. 40–71.

6. Central Committee of the CPA, "Statement of the CPA," p. 40.

7. The Alianza Popular Revolucionaria finished fourth in the elections of 11 March 1973 (with approximately 800,000 votes), behind the Peronists (approximately 6 million), the Radicals (about 2.5 million), and the Alianza Popular Federalista (about 1.8 million).

8. Central Committee of the CPA, "Communist party will take a positive stand on the new government," p. 31–32.

9. Ibid., p. 33.

10. Fourteenth Congress of the CPA, "Political resolution," p. 6.

11. Arnedo Alvarez, "Unidos por una nueva Argentina liberada." Report given to the Fourteenth Congress of the CPA, in *Cuatro décadas,* pp. 119–22, 133–34.

12. Communist criticism of Perón and Peronism was frequent from 1943 on. For more recent examples—made before the tactical shift in support of the last Peronist government—see Ghioldi, "El Peronismo y los problemas." See also Nadra, *Perón, hoy y ayer.*

13. Arnedo Alvarez, "Hacia donde marchan los acontecimientos políticos en la Argentina." Report to the Central Committee of the CPA, 15, 16 December 1973, in *Cuatro décadas,* p. 175.

14. CPA, "The people can win."

15. Executive Committee of the CPA, "The decisive moment draws nearer."

16. CPA Executive Committee, "Communist party's reply to the 'Rodrigo Plan,'" p. 73.

17. Ibid., p. 76.

18. Central Committee of the CPA, "Eighth National Conference of the CPA (December 1975)," p. 13.

19. Central Committee of the CPA, "The communists and the new situation in Argentina." p. 39.

20. See Organization of American States, Interamerican Commission on Human Rights, *Report.*

21. Graham-Yool, *The Press in Argentina,* p. 120.

22. Arnedo Alvarez et al., "Stop the political terror," p. 49.

23. Ghioldi et al., "Building a renovated democracy." Argentinian Communists, "The people came out for a dialogue and democratization"; "For national unity, toward a renovated democracy."

24. Arnedo Alvarez, "The political situation in Argentina."

25. Arnedo Alvarez, "Our proposals to the nation."

26. *Noticias Argentinas,* 4 July 1980.

27. Pascual Albanese, "Nueva conducción no cambiará la orientación del PCA," p. 10.

28. Ibid.

29. Iscaro, "Concerted action: assurance of success," p. 48.

30. *Buenos Aires Herald,* 11 February 1981.

31. Orestes Ghioldi, "En el complicado proceso de la Argentina," pp. 94, 100.

32. Fava, "Unidad y lucha."

33. MTI (Budapest), 16 September 1981.

34. Arnedo Alvarez, "Argentina y el mundo actual," pp. 13–17.

35. Fava, broadcast on "Semana Argentina" (Moscow), 23 April 1982; *Sovetskaya Rossiya,* 6 May 1982.

36. See República Argentina, Ministerio de Economía, Hacienda y Fínanzas, *Anuario estadístico,* pp. 523–25.

37. Ibid.

38. See International Monetary Fund, *Direction of Trade,* published annually, for the relevant years.

39. Ibid.

40. *Dinámica rural, edición especial: Comercio de granos,* pp. 20–21.

41. Iriarte, "El mercado de carne vacuna," p. 12.

42. Ibid., p. 15.

43. *Somos,* no. 241 (1 May 1981): 46–48; *Clarín,* 8, 10, 17 19 May 1981.

44. For a description of the global effects of the neoliberal economic policy adopted by the military government after 1976, see Canitrot, *La disciplina como objetivo* and "Teoría y práctica del liberalismo." For the postulates that guided this policy, see República Argentina, Ministerio de Economía, *Memoria.*

45. *Los Andes,* 12, 16, 17 May 1981.

46. See República Argentina, Ministerio de Economía, Hacienda y Finanzas, *Información económica de la Argentina,* no. 119 (July–August 1981).

47. See Kubalkova and Cruickshank, *Marxism-Leninism,* pp. 158–67.

48. See statements by Stalin in *Pravda,* February 1951, cited in Clissold, *Soviet Relations,* p. 157.

49. See statements by Bulganin in *Vision,* January 1956, in Clissold, *Soviet Relations,* pp. 158–59.

Bibliography

• *Books*

Alexander, Robert. *Communism in Latin America*. New Brunswick, N.J.: Rutgers University Press, 1957.

Amaral, Edgardo L. *Anecdotario de Lisandro de la Torre y debate sobre el comunismo*. Buenos Aires: Comísión Nacional de Homenaje a Lisandro de la Torre, 1957.

Arnedo Alvarez, Gerónimo. *Cuatro décadas de los procesos políticos argentinos, selección de trabajos*. Buenos Aires: Fundamentos, 1978.

Arriagada, Genaro. *Ideology and Politics in the South American Military (Argentina, Brazil, Chile, and Uruguay)*. Washington: The Wilson Center, Latin American Program, Working Paper No. 55, 1979.

Bagú, Sergio. *Argentina en el mundo*. Mexico City: FCE, 1961.

Braden, Spruille. *Diplomats and Demagogues*. New York: Arlington House, 1971.

Braun, Oscar, comp. *El capitalismo argentino en crisis*. Buenos Aires: Siglo XXI, 1973.

Bravo, Edgar R. *The Soviet View of the Latin American Military Regimes*, Ph.D. diss., University of Miami, 1978.

Cámpora, Héctor J. *La revolución peronista*. Buenos Aires: Eudeba, 1973.

Canitrot, Adolfo. *La disciplina como objetivo de la política económica. Un ensayo sobre el programa económico del gobierno argentino desde 1976*. Buenos Aires: Estudios CEDES, No. 6, 1979.

CEPAL. *Recopilación de convenios, acuerdos y protocolos vigentes*. Santiago de Chile: E/CEPAL/PROY. 4/R.14, November 1979.

CEPAL. *Relaciones económicas entre América Latina y los países miembros del CAME, informe de la secretaría de CEPAL*. Santiago de Chile: E/CEPAL/G. 1104. May 1980.

Cheston, T. Stephen. *Diplomatic Sideshow: A Study of Soviet Relations with Latin America, 1918–1936*. Ph.D. diss., Georgetown University, 1972.

Clark, Ronald. *Latin American Economic Relations with the Soviet Bloc, 1954–1961*. Ph.D. diss., Indiana University, 1963.

Clissold, Stephen. *Soviet Relations with Latin America*. London: Oxford University Press, 1970.

Conil Paz, Alberto, and Gustavo Ferrari. *Argentina's Foreign Policy, 1930–1962*. South Bend, Ind.: University of Notre Dame Press, 1966.

Deheza, José. *Marzo 23, hora 24*. Buenos Aires: Edición del Autor, 1977.

• *143*

Díaz Araujo, Enrique. *La conspiración del 43. EL GOU: una experiencia militarista en la Argentina,* Buenos Aires: La Bastilla, 1971.

Echague, Carlos. *El otro imperialismo en nuestra patria.* Buenos Aires: Ediciones de mayo, 1977.

Estremadoyro, Enrique. *Relaciones económicas de Argentinos con los países miembros del Consejo de Asistencia Mutua Económica (CAME).* Santiago de Chile: E/CEPAL/ PROY. 4/R.3, Noviembre 1979.

Ferrer, Aldo. *La economía Argentina.* Mexico City: FCE, 1963.

Frondizi, Arturo. *Petróleo y política.* Buenos Aires: Raigal, 1956.

Graham-Yool, Andrew. *The Press in Argentina, 1973–1978.* London: Writers and Scholars Educational Trust, Index on Censorship, 1979.

Green, David. *The Containment of Latin America.* Chicago: Quadrangle Books, 1971.

Hamburg, Roger P. *The Soviet Union and Latin America, 1953–1963.* Ph. D. diss., University of Wisconsin, 1965.

Irazusta, Julio. *Influencia económica británica en el Río de la Plata.* Buenos Aires: Eudeba, 1973.

Kossarev, Evgueni. *Relaciones económicas entre los países de América Latina y los países miembros del Consejo de Asistencia Mutua Económica (CAME).* Santiago de Chile, E/CEPAL/PROY. 4/R.16, November 1979.

Kubálková, V., and A. A. Cruickshank. *Marxism-Leninism and the Theory of International Relations.* London: Routledge and Kegan Paul, 1980.

Lanusse, Alejandro A. *Mi testimonio.* Buenos Aires: Lasserre, 1977.

Luder, Italo. *Argentina en Latinoamerica y en el mundo.* Buenos Aires: Eudeba, 1976.

Luna, Félix. *De Perón a Lanusse.* Buenos Aires: Planeta, 1975.

————. *El 45: Crónica de un año decisivo.* Buenos Aires: Jorge Alvarez, 1969.

————. *Yrigoyen.* Buenos Aires: Desarrollo, 1964.

Marini, Alberto. *Estrategia sin tiempo: La guerra subversiva y revolucionaria.* Buenos Aires: Círculo Militar-Biblioteca del Oficial, 1971.

Morgan, Dan. *Merchants of Grain.* Harmondsworth, Middlesex: Penguin, 1980.

Muñiz Ortega, Carlos. *La URSS y América Latina. 50 años de relaciones diplomáticas y económicas.* Lima: Moncloa, 1968.

Nadra, Fernando. *Perón, hoy y ayer (1971–1943).* Buenos Aires: Anteo, 1972.

Organization of American States, Interamerican Commission on Human Rights. *Report on the Situation of Human Rights in Argentina.* Washington, D.C.: OAS, 1980.

Oswald, Gregory, and Anthony Stover, eds. *The Soviet Union and Latin America.* New York: Praeger, 1974.

Parkinson, P. *Latin America, the Cold War, and the World Powers, 1945–1973.* Beverly Hills, Calif.: Sage, 1974.

Partido Comunista Argentino. *Esbozo de historia del Partido Comunista de la Argentina.* Buenos Aires: Anteo, 1947.

Perón, Juan Domingo. *Doctrina peronista.* Buenos Aires: Ediciones del Pueblo, 1971.

Potash, Robert. *El ejército y la política en la Argentina, 1928–1943 (De Yrigoyen a Perón).* Buenos Aires: Sudamericana, 1971.

————. *The Army and Politics in Argentina, 1945–1962.* Stanford, Calif.: Stanford University Press, 1980.

Ramos, Jorge A. *Historia del stalinismo en la Argentina.* Buenos Aires: Rancagua, 1974.

Redacción "Ciencias sociales contemporáneas." *Relaciones Soviético-Latinoamericanas (Recopilación de Documentos),* vol. 1. Moscow: USSR Academy of Science, 1981.

República Argentina, Ministerio de Agricultura y Ganadería, Junta Nacional de Granos. *Anuario 1981.*

República Argentina, Ministerio de Economía. *Boletín Semanal de Economía.*

————. *Memoria (29-3-1976/29-3-1981).* 3 vols. Buenos Aires, 1981.

República Argentina, Ministerio de Economía, Hacienda y Finanzas. *Anuario Estadístico 1979–1980.*

República Argentina, Secretaría de Estado de Agricultura y Ganadería, Junta Nacional de Carnes. *Síntesis Estadística: Año 1972.*

Rouquié, Alain. *Pouvoir militaire et société politique en République Argentine.* Paris: Presses de la fondation nationale des sciences politiques, 1978.

Ruiz Moreno. *Historia de las relaciones exteriores Argentinas (1810–1955).* Buenos Aires, Perrot, 1961.

Scalabrini Ortiz, Raúl. *Política británica en el Río de la Plata.* Buenos Aires: Plus Ultra, 1973.

Scenna, Miguel A. *Argentina-Brasil: Cuatro siglos de rivalidad.* Buenos Aires: La Bastilla, 1975.

Schillizzi Moreno, Horacio A. *Argentina contemporánea: Fraude y entrega, 1930–1943,* 2, vols. Buenos Aires: Plus Ultra, 1973.

Selser, Gregorio. *El Onganiato,* vols. 1, 2. Buenos Aires: Carlos Samonta, 1973.

Sobel, Lester, ed. *Argentina and Perón: 1970–75.* New York: Facts on File, 1975.

Stoetzer, Oto. *Two Studies on Contemporary Argentine History.* New York: Argentina Independent Review, 1980.

Tomberg, Romuald G. *Relaciones económicas de la Unión Soviética con países de América Latina.* Santiago de Chile: E/CEPAL/PROY.4/r.12, November 1979.

Vacs, Aldo C. *La Unión Cívica Radical: Su papel en el sistema político argentino.* Mendoza: CRESO, 1978.

Varas, Augusto. *América Latina y La Unión Soviética: Relaciones interestatales y vínculos políticos.* Santiago de Chile: FLASCO, Documento de Trabajo, no. 24, 1981.

Villegas, Osiris. *Guerra revolucionaria comunista.* Buenos Aires: Círculo Militar-Biblioteca del Oficial, 1962.

Wynia, Gary W. *Argentina in the Postwar Era. Politics and Economic Policy Making in a Divided Society.* Albuquerque: University of New Mexico Press, 1978.

• *Articles*

Albanese, Pascual. "Nueva conducción no cambiará la orientación del PCA." *Convicción,* 16 July 1980, p. 10.

146 • Bibliography

"América Latina: Política exterior y dependencia económia," *América Latina*, nos. 10–12 (1981).

Argentinian Communists. "For national unity, toward a renovated democracy." *World Marxist Review Publications Information Bulletin*, no. 364 (1978): 24–27.

————. "The people come out for a dialogue and democratization." *World Marxist Review Publications Information Bulletin*, no. 345 (1977): 19–20.

Arnedo Alvarez, Gerónimo. "Argentina y el mundo actual." *América Latina*, no. 2 (1978): 27–48.

————. "Our proposals to the nation." *World Marxist Review Publications Information Bulletin*, no. 404 (1979): 28–33.

————. "The political situation in Argentina." *World Marxist Review Publications Information Bulletin*, no. 380 (1979): 37–40.

Arnedo Alvarez, Gerónimo, et al. "Stop the political terror." *World Marxist Review Publications Information Bulletin*, no. 324 (1976): 49–50.

Baryshev, Alexander, "Argentina: Pressing problems." *New Times*, no. 39 (September 1979): 12–13.

————. "In search of a way out." *New Times*, no. 51 (December 1977): 22–24.

Belnap, David. "Argentina warms up to Soviet ties." *Los Angeles Times*, 25 August 1979, p. 4.

Bono, Agostino. "Argentina makes aggressive comeback in world wheat trade, at expense of U.S." *Wall Street Journal*, 7 March 1977, p. 22.

"Bunge is a worldwide concern that is shrouded in mystery." *New York Times*, 25 June 1957, p. 18.

Canitrot, Adolfo. "Teoría y práctica del liberalismo. Política antiinflacionaria y apertura económica en la Argentina, 1976–1981." *Desarrollo Económico* 21, no 82 (July-September 1981): 131–89.

Castro, Fidel, "Misión Gelbard: El fin del cerco." *Crisis*, no. 14 (June 1974): 3–8.

Central Committee of the Communist Party of Argentina. "Communist party will take a positive stand on the new government." *World Marxist Review Publications Information Bulletin*, no. 239 (1973): 31–37.

————. "Eighth National Conference of the CPA (December 1975)," *World Marxist Review Publications Information Bulletin*, no. 304 (1975): 13.

————. "The communists and the new situation in Argentina." *World Marxist Review Publications Information Bulletin*, no. 311 (1976): 36–40.

————. "The dictatorship's 'political plan' and the communist position." *World Marxist Review Publications Information Bulletin*, nos. 202–03 (1971): 24–30.

————. "Statement of the CPA." *World Marxist Review Publications Information Bulletin*, no. 325 (1973): 39–41.

————. "Unity and the struggle against the dictatorship for an anti-imperialist, popular, and democratic solution in Argentina." *World Marxist Review Publications Information Bulletin*, nos. 224–25 (1972): 40–49.

Chirkov, Vladislav. "Coup that was expected." *New Times*, no. 14 (April 1976): 10–11.

Communist Party of Argentina. "For a democratic national life: For the national and social liberation of the Argentine people." *World Marxist Review Publications Information Bulletin,* nos. 216–17 (1972): 66–69.

————. "The people can win." *World Marxist Review Publications Information Bulletin,* no. 272 (1974): 35–36.

Dinámica rural, edición especial: Comercio de granos (Buenos Aires), no. 145 (November 1980): 20–21.

Economic Information on Argentina. Coordination and Planning Secretariat, [Argentine] Ministry of Economy, no. 97 (June 1979): 24–28.

Executive Committee of the Communist Party of Argentina. "Communist party's reply to the 'Rodrigo Plan.'" *World Marxist Review Publications Information Bulletin,* nos. 292–93 (1975): 73–76.

————. "The decisive moment draws nearer." *World Marxist Review Publications Information Bulletin,* no. 274 (1974): 21–24.

Fava, Athos. "Unidad y lucha: Garantía de una apertura democrática." *América Latina* 42, no. 9 (1981): 27–48.

————. Interview on Radio Moscow. "Semana Argentina," 23 April 1982.

Ferrer, Aldo. "El retorno del liberalismo: Reflexiones sobre la política económica vigente en la Argentina." *Desarrollo Económico* 18, no. 72 (January–March 1979): 485–510.

Fichet, Gerard. "Tres decenios de relaciones entre América Latina y la Unión Soviética." *Comercio Exterior* 31, no. 2 (1981): 160–69.

Fourteenth Congress of the Communist Party of Argentina. "Political resolution." *World Marxist Review Publications Information Bulletin,* no. 251 (1973): 5–12.

Ghioldi, Orestes. "En el complicado proceso de la Argentina las masas tendrán la última palabra." *América Latina,* nos. 37–38 (1981): 89–100.

Ghioldi, Rodolfo. "El peronismo y los problemas de la lucha de las fuerzas progresistas para la creación de un Frente Unido." *Latinskaya América,* November–December 1972, pp. 66–79; January–February 1973, pp. 63–79.

Ghioldi, Rodolfo, et al. "Building a renovated democracy." *World Marxist Review Publications Information Bulletin,* no. 338 (1977): 19–23.

Iriarte, Ignacio. "El mercado de carne vacuna: Situación actual y perspectivas para 1981." *Convenio-Información Económica* 3, no. 18 (February 1981): 1–18.

Iscaro, Rubens. "Concerted action: Assurance of success." *World Marxist Review* 23 (December 1980): 48–51.

Karmen, A., "Military Junta in Power." *Komsomolskaya Pravda,* 26 March 1976, p. 3.

Kosichev, Leonard. "Argentina: Troubled times." *New Times,* no. 43 (October 1974): 10–11.

Landi, Oscar. "Argentina 1973–1976: La génesis de una nueva crisis política." *Revista Mexicana de Sociología* 41 (1979): 89–127.

————. "La tercera presidencia de Perón: Gobierno de emergencia y crisis política." *Revista Mexicana de Sociología* 40 (1978): 1353–1410.

Leiken, Robert S. "Eastern winds in Latin America." *Foreign Policy,* no. 42 (Spring 1981): 94–113.

Lozza, Arturo. "Whither Argentina?" *New Times*, no. 32 (August 1976): 24–26.

Maksinenko, L. "Coup d'état in Argentina." *Pravda*, 25 March 1976, p. 5.

Onis, Juan de. "Record Argentine harvest." *New York Times*, 14 March 1977, p. 43.

Orlov, P. "Soviet-Argentine relations: New stage." *New Times*, no. 20 (May 1974): 6–7.

Portantiero, Juan C. "Economía y política en la crisis argentina: 1958–1973." *Revista Mexicana de Sociología* 30 (1977): 531–65.

Robbins, William. "Inquiry widening on grain exports." *New York Times*, 25 June 1975, pp. 1, 18.

Seryogin, Y. "Argentina: Confrontation of the forces of democracy and reaction." *International Affairs*, no. 11 (November 1974), pp. 77–85.

Simorra, Boris. "Argentine Tango." *New Times*, no. 15 (April 1977): 28–30.

Smirnov, Alexander. "Who's stirring up trouble at Cape Horn?" *New Times*, no. 48 (November 1978): 26–27.

Tereknov, G. "Soviet-Argentine trade relations." *Foreign Trade*, no. 6 (June 1974): 14–15.

Tuzmujavédov, Rais. "La no alineación: ¿Etapa latinoamericana?" *Panorama Latinoamericano: Boletín Quincenal de la Agencia de Prensa Novosti*, no. 143 (March 1972): 1–21.

Zinovyev, N. "Soviet economic links with Latin America." *International Affairs*, no. 1 (January 1981): 100–07.

• *Periodicals, Newspapers, and News Services*

Argentina

Buenos Aires Herald
Clarín
Confirmado
Dinámica Rural
El Economista
Información Económica de la Argentina
La Nación
La Opinión
La Prensa
Los Andes
Mercado
Noticias Argentinas (news service)
Novedades de la Unión Soviética
Somos
TELAM (news service)
Ultima Clave

USSR

América Latina
Foreign Trade
International Affairs
Izvestiya
Komsomolskaya Pravda
New Times
Panorama Latinoamericano: Boletín Quincenal de la Agencia de Prensa Novosti
Pravda
"Semana Argentina" (radio program)
Sovetskaya Rossiya
TASS (news service)
World Marxist Review
World Marxist Review Publishers Information Bulletin

United States

Christian Science Monitor
Journal of Commerce
Los Angeles Times
Miami Herald
Newsweek
New York Times
The World Today
Wall Street Journal
Washington Post

Great Britain

Financial Times
Latin American Commodities Report
Latin American Political Report

Other Countries

El Día (Uruguay)
El Mercurio (Chile)
MTI (news service, Hungary)

Index

Aeroflot, 34, 57
Aerolíneas Argentinas, 34, 57
AFNE (Astilleros y Fabricaciones
  Navales del Estado), 56, 64
Agreements, Argentine-Soviet: on agri-
  cultural products, xvii, 33, 36–37, 49,
  51, 52–55; on economic-commercial
  and scientific-technological coopera-
  tion, 31–32, 44; on machinery and
  equipment, xvii–xviii, 18–19, 32, 39,
  44–45; on maritime transportation, 36,
  53–54; on trade and payments, 15–16,
  17, 26–27
Agua y Energía Eléctrica, 39, 42, 57, 107
Aguado, Jorge, 109
Air incident (1981), 81–82
Aleman, Juan, 102
Allende, Salvador, 25, 66, 68, 96
Alvear, Marcelo T. de, 5
Amtorg, 4
Antartic Treaty Consultative Meeting, 81
Anticommunism: of Argentine business
  groups, 106, 109, 123, 126; of Argentine civilian governments, xvii, 5, 10,
  14–15, 93, 95, 97, 116–17, 126; of
  Argentine military, xvii, 6–7, 10,
  18–19, 22–23, 27–28, 42, 67, 87,
  93, 94, 98, 117–18, 126
Arcos, 4
Argentine-Soviet chamber of commerce,
  30–31
Argentine-Soviet joint commission: crea-
  tion of, 34; first meeting of, 36–37;
  second meeting of, 42–43; third meeting of, 44; fourth meeting of, 51; fifth

  meeting of, 53; sixth meeting of,
  55–57
Arnedo Alvarez, Gerónimo, 95, 99, 100
Atucha I, 52, 89, 90. *See also* Nuclear
  cooperation
Atucha II, 89. *See also* Nuclear cooperation

Bameule, Luis, 63
Beagle Channel dispute, 25, 77, 88
Bolsa de Cereales de Buenos Aires, 106
Braden, Spruille, 11
Braiko, Ivan Yacovich, 87
Bramuglia, Juan Atilio, 13, 14
Bravo, Leopoldo, 15, 52, 76–77, 82
Brezhnev, Leonid, 33, 69, 83
Brutants, Karen, 103
Buenos Aires Herald, 63
Bulganin, Nikolai, 111

Cafiero, Antonio, 38
Cámara Argentina de Frigoríficos Indus-
  triales y Exportadores de Carne, 106
Camilión, Oscar, 81
Cámpora, Hector J., 28, 68, 95, 96
Cantilo, Jose María, 10
Cantoni, Federico, 13
Capellini, Orlando, 87
CARBAP (Confederacion de Asocia-
  ciones Rurales de Buenos Aires y La
  Pampa), 106, 109
Carter, James, 48, 74, 78, 79
Castillo, Ramón S., 9, 10
Castro Madero, Carlos, 55, 90
Chicherin, G. V., 3
Clarín, 62

PITT LATIN AMERICAN SERIES
Cole Blasier, Editor

U.S. Policies

CUBA, CASTRO, AND THE UNITED STATES
Philip W. Bonsal

THE HOVERING GIANT: U.S. RESPONSES TO REVOLUTIONARY CHANGE IN LATIN AMERICA
Cole Blasier

ILLUSIONS OF CONFLICT: ANGLO-AMERICAN DIPLOMACY TOWARD LATIN AMERICA
Joseph Smith

PUERTO RICO AND THE UNITED STATES, 1917–1933
Truman R. Clark

THE UNITED STATES AND CUBA: HEGEMONY AND DEPENDENT DEVELOPMENT, 1880–1934
Jules Robert Benjamin

Social Security

THE POLITICS OF SOCIAL SECURITY IN BRAZIL
James M. Malloy

SOCIAL SECURITY IN LATIN AMERICA: PRESSURE GROUPS, STRATIFICATION, AND INEQUALITY
Carmelo Mesa-Lago

Argentina

ARGENTINA IN THE TWENTIETH CENTURY
David Rock, Editor

DISCREET PARTNERS: ARGENTINA AND THE USSR SINCE 1917
Aldo César Vacs

JUAN PERÓN AND THE RESHAPING OF ARGENTINA
Frederick C. Turner and José Enrique Miguens, Editors

Brazil

THE POLITICS OF SOCIAL SECURITY IN BRAZIL
James M. Malloy

URBAN POLITICS IN BRAZIL: THE RISE OF POPULISM, 1925–1945
Michael L. Conniff

Colombia

GAITÁN OF COLOMBIA: A POLITICAL BIOGRAPHY
Richard E. Sharpless

ROADS TO REASON: TRANSPORTATION, ADMINISTRATION, AND RATIONALITY IN COLOMBIA
Richard E. Hartwig

Cuba

ARMY POLITICS IN CUBA, 1898–1958
Louis A. Pérez, Jr.

CUBA BETWEEN EMPIRES, 1878–1902
Louis A. Pérez, Jr.